GLASS:
A Guide for Collectors

Spirit flask, South German, *c.* 1775, perhaps Fichtelgebirge, cold enamelled. Ht. 14 cm.; and large flared beaker, Bohemian, cold enamelled, 1678, showing Eve tempting Adam. Ht. 16·5 cm.

GABRIELLA GROS-GALLINER

GLASS:
A Guide for Collectors

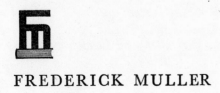

FREDERICK MULLER

First published in Great Britain 1970
by Frederick Muller Ltd., Fleet Street, London, E.C.4

Copyright © 1970 Gabriella Gros-Galliner

748
191628 ₒᴫ

Printed in Great Britain
by Ebenezer Baylis and Son, Ltd.
The Trinity Press, Worcester, and London
Bound by G. & J. Kitcat Ltd.
SBN: 584 10107 4

CONTENTS

ILLUSTRATIONS

Colour Plates

Monochrome Plates

Line Illustrations

ACKNOWLEDGEMENTS

In the course of preparing this book, I have met with innumerable kindnesses from fellow collectors and museum curators. In the first instant, my appreciation and thanks go to Dr. E. Launert for reading the manuscript, discussing relevant points and making many interesting and helpful observations and suggestions. I am also indebted to him for allowing me to reproduce glass from his personal collection. My gratitude is due to those private collectors who have not only permitted me to show some of their fine glass in this book but have also generously entrusted me with some of their precious pieces for photographic purposes. Mr. R. J. Charleston, Keeper of Ceramics at the Victoria and Albert Museum, has been kind enough to loan photographs from the Museum's own files (plates facing pp. 33, left; 49, top; 81, left; 112, bottom) and Dr. Ada Polak the photograph (plate facing p. 96, right) reproduced in her book *Gammelt Norsk Glass* (Oslo, 1953). Further thanks are due to Mr. Hugh Tait of the Department of British and Medieval Antiquities, at the British Museum, for his assistance in obtaining the illustrations from the Museum Catalogue, and to Miss Wendy Evans of the Glass Manufacturers' Federation for checking some of the bibliographical references. I am also most grateful to Mr. Paul N. Perrot, Director of the Corning Museum of Glass, N.Y., for making available the photographs of American glass and arranging for such detailed descriptions. Messrs. Christie and Messrs. Sotheby have been good enough to supply and allow reproduction of photographs from their catalogues.

The Plates:

By courtesy of the British Museum: plates facing pp. 16; 17 top; 32; 33 right; 48 right; 64 top; 65; 72; 80 top; 81 right; 96 left; 128 top and plate between pp. 72–73 inside left.

By courtesy of the Corning Museum of Glass, Corning, N.Y., U.S.A.: plates facing pp. 145, top left and right; 160; 161.

By courtesy of the Fitzwilliam Museum, Cambridge: plate facing p. 33, left.

By courtesy of the Kunstindustri Museet, Oslo: plate facing p. 96, right.

By courtesy of the Pilkington Glass Museum, St. Helens, Lancs.: plate facing p. 49 top.

By courtesy of Messrs. Christie, Manson & Woods Ltd.: plates facing pp. 80 bottom; 97 bottom.

By courtesy of Messrs. Sotheby & Co.: plates facing pp. 48 left; 49 bottom; 64 bottom; 97 top; 112 top.

By courtesy of Leslie Scott: frontispiece, right; plates facing pp. 88; 120 left.

From the following collections:

A. J. B. Kiddell, Esq.: plate facing p. 112, bottom.

Dr. E. Launert: frontispiece, left; plates facing pp. 40; 113; 128 bottom.

Mrs. Paul Rothschild: plates facing pp. 17 bottom; 129 top; 144 top, nos. 2 and 3; 144 bottom, no. 4.

J. S. M. Scott, Esq.: plate facing p. 73.

Gabriella Gros: plates facing p. 17 bottom (beads only); 120 nos. 2 and 3; 129 bottom; 144 top no. 1; 144 bottom nos. 1, 2, 3, 5; 145 bottom; plate between pp. 72–73 inside right.

Glass furnace from Georgius Agricola's
De Re Metallica, 1556

1
Historical Highlights

The intention of this chapter is not to burden the reader with historical details but to convey within an acceptable frame an overall picture of some of the more important developments of glass making, particularly in its early stages.

The development of any form of art, its flowering and decline, is conditioned not only by attribute of national characteristics but by geographical, historical and economic factors. Against such influences, whether of political or domestic nature, beneficial or detrimental, the individual is powerless. Were this not the case we should be left with a heritage possibly akin to a form of folk-art of uneven merit, produced in a concentrated area, modelling itself on examples of earlier generations, and devoid of the spirit of invention and enterprise.

Seen in perspective, glass history might be represented as a gigantic piece of mosaic with its most brilliantly coloured pieces spaced as widely apart as East and West, a number of poorly coloured areas reflecting very little light, and some entirely empty spaces where the original pieces have been lost, perhaps for ever. It emerges quite clearly, however, that the invention of glass or, more properly, the art of glazing—of which glass is a further stage—is of the greatest antiquity. Moreover, by the time Christ was born, use was being made of every decorative technique known to us today, with the exception of acid etching, sand blasting and certain methods of pressing which are modern. The oldest glass finds we know were made in the Tigris–Euphrates region and their date of manufacture is ascribed to a period near 2500 B.C. For the next thousand years we are left in darkness as to the fate of the glassmaker's art, but from 1500 B.C. we can trace an increasingly flourishing industry throughout the Eastern

Mediterranean area. Pliny, Herodotus and Thephrastus are unanimous in their praise of the glass industries at Thebes, Sidon, Tyre and Alexandria.

Basically, glass is an artificial material derived from the fusion of silica (sand, flint or quartz) with an alkaline flux—soda or potash. Soda was obtained by burning seaweed or other marine plants. Potash is a product of wood ash. Broadly speaking, therefore, industries situated on or near the coast used soda in the making of their glass-products, whereas potash was favoured for inland manufacture. The advantages of the geographical location of ancient glass centres in the Mediterranean littoral are self-evident. The River Belus was one of the main sources of the sand which contributed so much to the fame of Phoenician glass. In 1322 the great traveller Sir John Mandeville told of this sand still being used: "Men comen fro fer watre by shippes and be londe with cartes, to fetchen of that gravelle." Moses is assumed to have known of this river when blessing Zebulun and Issachar and saying that 'they shall suck of the abundance of the seas and of treasures hid in the sand.' It is quite possible he was referring to glass and no doubt he was familiar with the processes of its manufacture. The ancient Hebrews acquired their knowledge of glassmaking from the Egyptians and Phoenicians. They practised their craft in their homeland, in Syria and, being perforce a migratory people, in their foreign settlements. Their wandering took them, as well as artisans of other semitic races such as the Syrians, to Italy, Gaul, across the Alps to the Rhine areas and to Spain. Illuminated Hebrew manuscripts of the early Middle Ages show Jewish ritual objects made of glass—chalices and lamps—lamps similar in design to the later Islamic mosque type. Solomon and the King of Tyre, which was renowned for its glass industry, were on the friendliest of terms. We are all familiar with the story of the Queen of Sheba's visit to King Solomon. Crossing the forecourt to the Palace, the beautiful Queen lifted the hem of her robe, for she imagined herself to be walking on a shallow pool of water. The King was delighted and explained to her that the floor was paved with glass.

After the defeat of the Persian army by Alexander in 333 B.C., Egypt, Babylon, Damascus and the other great cities of Palestine and Syria came under Greek domination and finally Gaza and Tyre submitted after fierce and long resistance. Under this Hellenistic influence all manner of inventive glass decoration flourished. A great wave of knowledge and enlightenment spread over the Hellenistic world, Alexandria became one of the most magnificent of trading cities and the established glassmaking centre of the Mediterranean. Cutting and coloured ornamentation was favoured and the Greek fashion of painting pottery vessels was echoed in the paintings on glass objects.

With the death of Alexander in 323 B.C. the dominion crumbled under the unstable rule of some of Alexander's greedy generals and a succession of weak, local controllers.

Rome had been putting out feelers for some expansion as early as the fifth century B.C. After the destruction of Carthage in 146 B.C. her military power began to be felt in the disorganized Mediterranean areas. In 26 B.C. Caesar Augustus demanded that glass should be part of the tribute paid by a subdued Egypt and for the next forty years Egyptian export trade in glass was at its height, a much-sought-after luxury for the wealthy Roman. By A.D. 1 glassmaking had become a highly developed craft of accomplished technique, blown glass began to replace the sand-core method and was introduced in Italy about A.D. 20. Under the prosperous and relatively peaceful conditions of the Roman Empire, the glassmakers, assimilated from diverse centres of Mediterranean glass industry, could and would wander about freely, often following in the wake of Roman occupation forces. The glass made during this period, termed 'Roman Glass', may well have been made by a Syrian in the Rhineland or an Alexandrian in Gaul and large quantities of glass were exported to the West, especially during the first centuries of Roman occupation. Glasshouses were in existence in Italy, Gaul and the German Rhineland until they, as so much else, were swept away by the Barbarians, this holocaust finally causing the disintegration of the Roman Empire. The Greek-speaking Eastern half of the Roman Empire was more tenacious in its efforts to survive. The 150 years following the Fall of Rome show a history of war and rivalry between the empires of Persia and Byzantium; however, the craft of glassmaking did not perish entirely as it had in the West. The adoption of Christianity as religion of State by Constantine inspired renewed and splendid achievements in the composition of pictures made of glass cubes, the *tesserae* or mosaics. The quiet colours of the Roman mosaic with its subdued background would have been insignificant on the walls of the grandly proportioned Byzantine basilica. A blaze of light and colour, and above all a radiance of gold, makes the Byzantine mosaic a fitting complement to decorate the splendid temples erected for worship of the new religion.

In 634 the Byzantine army was wiped out by Muslim forces at the battle of Yarmouk, and the next hundred years witnessed what must have been one of the greatest conquests of all time. Damascus, Palmyra, Antioch, Jerusalem, Persia, Western Turkestan and Egypt fell under the onslaught of the Arab attackers. The invaders streamed along the north coast of Africa, taking Spain and attempting to invade France, where they were finally halted at the battle of Poitiers. The mixed Arab tribes, which formed the nucleus of this new world power, had no particular artistic dexterity to their merit. In spite of this, and the throwing together of such vastly differing material, a distinct Islamic style emerged. Characteristic methods of decoration and individual design in decorative relief cutting remained the peculiarly Islamic trait of her glass industry for several centuries. From the twelfth century onward and well into the fifteenth the Islamic glass artists produced their finest achievement in their enamelled work, at its most splendid during A.D. 1250–1400.

Northern Europe in the meantime saw the establishment of a glass industry mainly created by Syrian glassmakers who settled in an area between the Seine and Rhine. The style which emerged was the result of a combined taste and conception of the Celtic and the oriental: Alexandrian-type coloured glass with northern decoration. Seine-Rhine glass, also referred to as Frankish or Rhenish, had its centres of industry in the areas of the Lorraine, Trèves, Picardy, Mainz, Cologne, Namur and Liège. Because glass production was scattered over a fairly wide area certain differences exist, but they are not sufficiently important to erase a unity of style. Glasswares from the Seine–Rhine glassfields were also exported to Britain and Scandinavia. The metal of this period is of attractive colour, blue, bluish-green, amber, and shows trailed, stuck- or dropped-on and thread decoration, distinctly Syrian or Semitic in conception. Drinking vessels became more enterprising in form and we may observe the evolution and perfection of the claw-beaker, particularly at the waning of Roman influence when, apart from the more domestic line, a certain quality glass was manufactured. During the sixth and seventh centuries a metal (the term used to signify the molten mass of glass) of liquid-greenish colour became prevalent in the forest regions where woodash was used as a source of potash alkali, the *Waldglas* or in France the *verre de fougère*, which can also have a pale amber tone.

In about A.D. 675 some French glassworkers are recorded to have arrived at Wearmouth, Durham, in order to make windows for the monastery there. Some eighty years later Abbot Cuthbert of this same monastery addressed a plea to Lullo, Bishop of Mainz, to send him if possible 'any man who can make vessels of glass well, for we are ignorant and helpless in that art.' For the preservation of the art of making coloured, painted and stained windowglass we are indebted to the Church and her monasteries. Windows of coloured glass are known to have existed in the sixth century A.D. and are of Eastern origin. The painted windows representing five prophets in the Augsburg Cathedral, Germany, are among the earliest known and date from the middle of the eleventh century. The *Diversarum Artium Schedulae*, written in the late eleventh century by Theophilus, a monk of Helmershausen in the diocese of Paderborn, and describing in the second volume the making of glass, glass vessels, glass rings and painted glass windows, seems to be a compilation of informative facts on the art of glassmaking as it had been practised for some time. Some of the stained glass for York Minster was made during the twelfth century. Laurence Vitrearius, a glassmaker from Normandy who settled at Dyers Cross near Pickhurst, supplied the stained glass windows for Westminster Abbey in 1240, probably from coloured glass imported from the Continent, and the great and beautiful stained glass windows of St. Chapelle, Chartres, date from the same period. The same century also witnessed the spectacular rise of Venice to a wealthy republic of unchallenged commercial and maritime power. After the sacking of Constantinople in 1204 the ambitious Venetians had assured themselves of some of the best Byzantine glassworkers. A very profitable industry was carried on in ornamental glassware, the export trade being enormously stimulated and expanded by the city's command of the north-to-south trade route.

In order to retain a future monopoly and to guard the city of Venice against possible danger of conflagration, the glass industry was moved to the island of Murano in 1291, separated from the city by a narrow strip of water. With the sacking of Damascus by Tamerlane in 1400 the Damascene glassmakers dispersed and their industry collapsed. Venice was well equipped to usurp Islam's hitherto undisputed position and to assume the role of the world's foremost glass industry herself. For the next two centuries, during the periods of the late Gothic and Renaissance/Baroque, glassmaking history is focused on Venice. It was an era of imaginative and inventive splendour, due in some part to the rediscovery of ancient glass-working methods and forms of decoration—millefiori, a descendant of the Roman murrhine, and the vitro-di-trina (lace glass) for instance. Experiments culminated in the development of the Venetian 'cristallo', a clear and colourless metal similar to rock crystal. This was achieved by an addition of manganese, a process which had long been forgotten. The secrets of Venetian practices and glass compositions were strictly guarded and severe punishment and heavy restrictions were imposed on the Murano glaziers and their families. It was to be expected that foreign glass industries were desirous of procuring the Venetian processes, and the lure of better conditions and greater reward was successful temptation for several of the Murano workmen. The results present a fascinating history of intrigue and violence and initiated the production of glass in the *façon de Venise* at many important glass centres throughout Europe. Furthermore, glassworkers from the rival glass industry at l'Altare, near Genoa, were not subjected to the tyranny of Murano and were free to travel wherever they wished.

In 1567 the protestant Lorrainer Jean Carré, working both in London and in Alford, obtained a licence for the manufacture of glass 'for glazing such as is made in France, Burgundy and Lorraine'. Carré was responsible for bringing over Verzelini and several other Venetians for the purpose of producing cristallo glass. He died within a few months of Verzelini's arrival in England and the Italian glassmaker took over where Carré left

The Lycurgus cup with open-work figured frieze. Opaque
green with yellow patch, wine-coloured with amethyst patch
by transmitted light. Roman 4th century A.D. Ht. (incl. metal
rim of later date) : 16·5 cm.

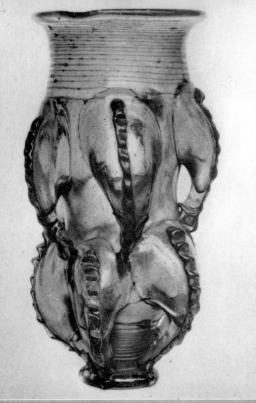

Left, a Rhenish claw beaker of the late 5th or early 6th century A.D. Green with royal blue over-trails. Ht. 19 cm.; *below, back row, left to right*, a cored Aryballos, Egypt. Dark blue, trailed and marvered decoration in yellow and light blue. 600–400 B.C. Ht. 6 cm.; a head flask, Sidon or Rome school. Greenish glass. A.D. 200–300. Ht. 7·5 cm.; English medicine bottles of the late 17th or early 18th century. Blue-green. Ht. 9 cm. and 6·5 cm.; *middle*, Roman blown-glass tear bottles. Ht. 8 cm., 6 cm. and 9 cm.; *front*, Egyptian and Alexandrian/Roman beads, some dating from 600 B.C.

off, establishing his glasshouse in 1573, not without some hindrance from local competition. As early as 1419 there is a record of an Italian glass-worker settling in Buda, Hungary, while in 1572 Fabriano Salviati of Murano began making glass in the Venetian style in Poitou near Poitiers. Antwerp was another city to attract Italian glassmakers and became one of the most active centres during the sixteenth century. While the glass manufactured by émigré Italian glassmakers has all the aspects of Vene-tian-inspired design, the metal does differ slightly in colour from the soda-cristallo glass produced in Venice from the late fifteenth century onward.

The next development heralding a new phase in glassmaking history was the 'Proclamation touching glasses', issued on May 23rd, 1615, and forbidding the use of wood fuel in the manufacture of glass. This act may be said to have invoked a whole string of consequences—coal furnaces were introduced, glass factories began to spring up in coalmining areas, and Mansell, who was the first Englishman to begin smelting with ordinary coal in 1635, used covered pots to protect the glass frit from the impurities resulting from coal dust. The temperature in these covered pots, however, was not sufficiently high for refining, and to make the pot metal more easily fusible a quantity of lead was added. This, so quotes a German source, led to the discovery of flintglass. Whether such an assumption can be substantiated or not, England had to wait a little longer for the inven-tion of lead crystal.

There had always been restrictions on the import of Venetian glass. In September 1635 Charles I granted a Charter to the London Glass Sellers Corporation and in 1640 they again imposed restrictions on the import of Venetian glass, a measure to foster and enlarge home trade and manu-facture. As we shall see later, the results were beneficial. The Company was reincorporated in 1664 as the 'Worshipful Company of Glass Sellers', an intelligent and powerful body, far-sighted and extremely competent commercially. In 1675 their membership numbered eighty-eight and, in principle, these were the men responsible for the development and supre-macy of English lead crystal.

George Ravenscroft (1618–81), a London shipowner and, as Mr. William A. Thorpe puts it, "a man of chemical interest", quite possibly had first-hand knowledge of the Murano glass industry. His interest in producing a "particular sort of christalline glass" caused the London Glass Sellers Company to engage him under contract and it appears that by 1676 Ravenscroft had overcome some of the difficulties that caused an effect of 'crizzling' or 'crisseling'. This was a general glass defect, due to excessive alkali contents and appearing as a fine network of minute interior cracks, resulting in deterioration and eventual disintegration of glass objects. The Company issued their famous 'First Certificate' dated June 3rd, 1676, declaring that a lead glass had now been perfected with complete success, and also making reference to the distinct ring of lead crystal, as opposed to soda glass. It was decided to mark this perfected metal with a seal— that of the Raven's Head. There is some proof that a type of lead glass was in varying experimental stages elsewhere, but it was not as consequential for glass development nor did it possess the quality that must be ascribed to the glass Ravenscroft invented, which underwent a continuing process of perfection long after his death in 1681. Ravenscroft's heritage has been preserved to the present day. No other foreign glass has quite the same lustrous quality of English lead crystal (pl. facing p. 49).

Pliny makes a reference to glass mirrors having been invented at Sidon. Four centuries earlier Aristotle wrote of polished metals and stones serving as mirrors and of glass and crystal being "lined with a sheet of metal to give back the image presented to them". Although in the fourteenth century this method is supposed to have been applied occasionally in Venice, mirrors of metal were in common usage. In 1507 two Murano glaziers, Andrea and Dominico d'Anzolo dal Gallo applied for, and were granted, the privilege of manufacturing mirrors of crystalline glass, a secret which they had learned from Germany and Flanders, where such mirrors were manufactured and exported. The new industry must have been successful for, in 1569 the *Specchiai*, or Mirror-makers, established their Guild. The history of mirror-making is one of secrets discovered by surreptitious spying and intrigue but it brought in its wake an invention of far greater importance—that of founding and casting glass of almost unlimited size. Baroque French taste, the result of which we may see at Versailles with its *Galerie des Glaces*, was becoming most demanding and extravagant and with the help of eighteen Venetian glassworkers a factory was established in 1665 in the Faubourg St. Antoine. The "Manufactory of Glass Mirrors by Venetian Workmen" was the incongruously uninspiring title for this establishment which was to furnish a luxury article for the elegant home. With the increasing demand for larger and better mirror glass it fell to a Frenchman, Louis Lucas de Nehou, to begin making glass by casting and in 1695 he installed his factory at St. Gobain. A little earlier, in 1664, the second Duke of Buckingham, George Villiers, who seems virtually to have had a finger in every pie, was granted the sole patent of manufacturing and importing mirror glass and in 1670 he founded the first factory of blown mirror glass at Lambeth.

Netherlandish glass development was influenced both by the émigré Venetians and the neighbouring German taste, producing Rœmers of relatively good quality, and fantastic shapes and creations that outshone even the Venetian 'flügel-glass'. Their greatest period comes with the decorative work carried out mainly in the eighteenth century. Dutch diamond stippling remains unsurpassed. For this type of decoration, Dutch glass quality was not entirely satisfactory and much of the artist's work was done on English glass vessels, imported mainly from the Newcastle area.

The Bohemians were more ambitious in their efforts to produce good and original glass. They have always been good technicians and the development of a more perfected glass furnace with grate is due to their ingenuity. The rise of Bohemian crystal began in the early seventeenth century, when the rediscovered method of engraving of the old lapidaries was applied to glass. Caspar Lehman (1570–1622), the exponent of Czech Baroque glass engraving, was a carver of precious stone at the Court of Rudolf II. This type of engraving was done at the wheel and the thin, brittle cristallo soda glass was not ideally suited for work requiring a more resistant, thick but clear metal. Eventually, in 1680, a successful glass composition was developed—the calcium potassic glass—and later the addition of lead produced a metal similar to Ravencroft's invention. The decorated and especially the cut glass of the eighteenth and early nineteenth centuries rank among Bohemia's finest contribution to the glassmaker's art. There was a revival of the early Christian *Zwischengold* (sandwich) glass method and the Biedermeier period brought a great vogue for intricately cut, engraved coloured glass, often overlaid or inset with panels of enamelled opaque white glass. The Biedermeier followed where the continental Empire style ended, about 1820–50. It is a word formed from the German, literally *Der biedere Meier*, a term describing the respectable bourgeois of comfortable means.

Glassmaking in neighbouring Germany and Austria developed on similar lines. Kunckel, a director of the Potsdam Glass Works, invented his famous gold-ruby glass in 1680, and Mildner (1763–1808), an Austrian working at Gutenbrunn, produced a distinctive variant of the Zwischengold glass method.

With the Baroque taste began the great period of English drinking-glasses. The desire for a more plastic expression of form was gratified, and stems, bowls and feet became of almost infinitely variable design. Proportion and shape were designed to satisfy a taste which was trying to break free from the restrictions of Gothic Renaissance and from Venetian influence. The development of the baluster was the glassmaker's reply to the plain and pleasant-to-look-at style of Queen Anne, and the variations of this trend showed incredible inventiveness. With the Rococo style, about the middle of the eighteenth century, there is reversion to colour and decorative glasswork, a light-hearted protest against the balanced design of the Baroque. The tax levied on glass by weight of ingredient in 1745–6 contributed to this movement; the need for less heavy articles conditioned a thinner glass. This called for shallower cutting, except perhaps on stems, and less engraving, but brought enamelling in the French Rococo taste such as was carried out by Edkins and the Beilbys. The Royalist movement brought with it the engraved glasses decorated with Jacobite emblems, one of the great delights of the collector of English drinking-glasses, as are the air and colour twists of the same period (plates facing p. 73).

A taste for the oriental became prevalent during the mid-decades of the eighteenth century and this phase of Rococo ornamentation, termed 'chinoiserie', affected arts and crafts alike—we need only think of 'Chinese Chippendale' and the Pagoda in Kew Gardens. This style, which persisted until the 'Biedermeier' period came to an end, was expressed in the forms and decorations of both china and glass and is reflected in the opaque white 'ginger jar' shape and coloured or gilt-decorated Bristol glass.

As a result of further Excise Acts in 1777, 1781 and 1787 English glass-workers began to establish some glasshouses in Ireland and enjoyed a substantial trade until 1825, when an Excise Duty was levied on Irish glass.

The Chinese are credited with a working knowledge of glass from about the third century A.D., but the finest and most artistically accomplished glassware was produced during the eighteenth century. It was cut and engraved in the manner of rock-crystal, and the snuff bottles for example, with their beautifully coloured and carved overlay glass, inspired the cameo-glass creations of Émile Gallé, at Nancy, a hundred years or so later (plate facing p. 144).

The first glass to be manufactured in America was made in 1608 at Jamestown, Virginia, the earliest permanent English settlement (May 14th, 1607). There was no successful glass industry until Caspar Wistar's factory was established in 1739, employing mainly Dutch workmen. In 1827 factories both at Cambridge and at Sandwich, Massachusetts, began experiments in pressing glass. A successful and highly efficient pressing-machine was developed which revolutionized glassmaking everywhere.

While the seedlings of Murano had so successfully enriched foreign soil the fortunes of Venice herself were dwindling. Continuous wars with Turkey had drained some of the city's greatest resources and with the discovery of the new trade route round the Cape of Good Hope there followed a decline in Venetian industrial achievement. She lost the all-important supremacy of the Mediterranean seas and in 1797, at the peace of Campo Formio, the republic was handed over to the Austrians by Napoleon. The *façon de Venise* had become outmoded and Venice lost a monopoly that had lasted for over two hundred years.

As the Baroque was a reaction to the severe splendour of the Renaissance, so the Classic, or Neo-classic, period developed, renouncing Rococo exuberance. There followed a reversion to heavier and plentiful cutting and consequently glass was again made of thicker and more brilliant metal. Use was made of ormolu and other metal mounts, there came a vogue for candelabra and chandeliers, covered goblets and urns in the Grecian style, and a tendency for large objects with a profusion of cut decoration leading into the Victorian age. There was certainly quantity and, even if style was often not too refined in taste, workmanship during the mid-nineteenth century was not lacking in quality.

Some caution must be exercised in using general terms to describe the art form of any one country. The true conception of Italian Baroque and French Rococo, for instance, has not inspired any equivalent response in England. The rise of the Byzantine Church brought a new, 'golden' splendour to the mosaic-maker's art. The Church of Rome built St. Peter's with its Baroque splendour. The gaily enamelled German Humpen, or tankards, of the seventeenth century stem from Bavaria and Franconia, and these same areas of Catholic concentration in Germany are jewel-studded with the sumptuous white and gold splendour of the late Baroque and Rococo periods. The Protestant Church in its sobriety did not support such frivolous artistic exuberance and consequently we also find in English glass of these periods a more subdued and realistic note. English enamelling of the Rococo period is often monochrome in tone. German and Bohemian 'Biedermeier' has no real equivalent in this country.

Ancient glass finds have been made in most of the Scandinavian countries. Attractive decorate glass of good quality was made in the eighteenth century and later, most of it foreign-influenced. Russia is only now beginning to tap her soil for ancient treasures. A fair amount of Syrian glass has been found at the ancient Crimean port of Kerch at the edge of the Black Sea and there are many reports of new finds in various areas. This is hardly surprising since the vast territory of the Soviet Union is traversed by ancient trade routes over land and water. There was some local industry of glazed tiles. Mosaics, coloured glass pictures and the enamelled decoration of the eighteenth century recall Byzantium and Islam. Nevertheless, at the time when we can speak of a Russian glass industry, that is to say the mid-1800s, the influence came not from the East but the West, from Paris and Potsdam. If we search for national character we might find it in contemporary glass—in the beautiful colours and clean lines of Scandinavian work, and the monumental architectural style of the U.S.S.R.

The period called 'Art Nouveau', which dates roughly from the late nineteenth century to about 1910–20, draws its inspiration from both East and West. It is the age of John Burckhardt's *Civilization of the Renaissance in Italy* (1878) and Bernard Berenson's reappraisal of Italian art. In the footsteps of the German School of the 'Nazarener' follow the English 'Pre-Raphaelites', and William Morris, the exponent of English Art Nouveau, is a direct product of this influence. This is the era of writhing plant forms and the trend for naturalistic expression, as interpreted by Émile Gallé in his glass creations and furniture designs. A flavour for the oriental is expressed in the softly bulbous shapes of glass and ceramic vases, and Joseph Brocard in Paris recaptured some of the splendour of Islamic glass art with his beautiful and sensitive enamelling of glass in the 'mosque-lamp style'. In odd contrast there is also a strange tendency toward Neo-gothic simplification of outline, a style recognisable in some of Tiffany's glass-pewter realizations.

Objectively seen, from the late seventeenth century onward there is an increasing tendency towards the decorative in glass art; the emphasis is not only on functionalism but on the aspect of visual enjoyment. Such aspirations imbue the final product with a more complex and individual character, which may differ according to its place of origin.

2

Glassmaking as a Craft

The glassmaker of today is expected to take full advantage of the advances made in modern science and technology to facilitate his work. The demand for and consequent production of all types of glass has increased beyond the wildest imagination of the early glassmakers. It is obvious that in order to satisfy demand and cope with competition the means of modern technology had to be applied to reduce wastage and improve efficiency of production. Some of the trial-and-error methods of the early glassmakers have given way to refined laboratory investigations and analyses. However, there is no short cut to true craftsmanship and the modern glassmaker will go through the same motions and apply the same tools to his craft as his ancestor centuries ago.

Quality, colour and character of the metal, that is to say, the molten mass of glass, are predetermined by the quantity and ratio of the components used. The main components of glass are silica, soda and lime. Due to its high melting point ($1710°C.$) pure silica is rarely used, except for the manufacture of glass with specific requirements. Experiments have recently been carried out to make a type of decorative glass from silica. It is most attractive to look at and has the natural feel and colours of stone or smooth rock, but is obviously expensive to produce. Depending on its location the glasshouse's source of soda was seaweed or other marine plants, or barillia, a type of kelp imported from Spain. In forest regions soda was substituted by potash derived from woodash. Beechwood was a favourite material and other woods used for this purpose were oak and, to a lesser extent, pinewood, as for instance in glass from the Fichtelgebirge. An important addition to the glassbatch is cullet, broken or waste pieces of glass often making up one-quarter and even one-half of the batch. Cullet was normally collected by the poor families and children of the surrounding areas who used it for barter or sold it back to the glasshouses. Re-use and collection of cullet is responsible for the poor yield of old glass on rediscovered glasshouse sites—a great source of disappointment for many a 'prospector'.

The mixture of raw materials and cullet is ground to form the glass frit (from *frittare*—to fry), ready for melting in the furnace. Cullet and frit were also more conveniently imported; the Seine–Rhine glassmakers imported both from the Eastern Mediterranean.

In physical terms glass is a super-cooled liquid because it has no crystalline structure and, without any definite melting point, will pass into a viscous fluid on heating. Melting of the frit is completed in three stages, the first consisting of placing or pouring it into the previously heated pot—a refractory crucible placed in the furnace. When fusion is complete, a sticky mass is obtained which is now ready for the second stage, namely that of refining. During this stage the temperature of the melt in the pot is increased considerably and reaches a maximum of 1600°C. This temperature causes the frit to become a thin liquid full of air bubbles, which rise and give off undesirable gases and vapour from water that may be contained in the sand. Other impurities also come to the surface and are skimmed off with the ladle. To complete the melting process it is necessary to cool the frit so that it may revert to its former sticky mass and be suitable for working. At this stage the metal will have a temperature around 700° or 800°C. and may be turned into any desired shape by blowing, moulding or pressing. Changes in the composition of the metal may take place in the furnace due to burn-up, absorption of the furnace lining components and slag formation. If the soda content of the melt is too high the viscosity of the liquid glass mass during cooling will be too high, i.e., it will be too thick and not flow easily. This can be remedied by adding more sand (silica) and results in a hard, transparent glass—waterglass—which is soluble in water, and may be remembered as the liquid used a few decades ago for preserving eggs. With the addition of lime we finally obtain the substance called glass, an artificial material which, after annealing, is strong, hard and durable. Annealing of the ready-shaped glass object is a process that has to be controlled very carefully and takes place in the annealing oven or lehr. Faulty annealing will affect and change the properties of the glass metal and often years may pass until such changes become apparent. The purpose of annealing is to reduce internal stresses which, if sufficiently great, may cause the glass to crack or break. A favourite demonstration of this property of glass is shown with the objects known as 'Prince Rupert's Drops'. These are tadpole-shaped glass drops, formed by dropping molten glass into water. There are high internal stress concentrations in the tail and if the tail is fractured the drop explodes into minute particles so that nothing but a fine powder will remain. Amusingly, Samuel Pepys reports on this experiment: "Mr. Peter did show us the experiment of the chymicall glasses which break all to dust by breaking off a little small end, which is a great mystery to me."

Today annealing ovens are automatically controlled but in early times the success of annealing was dependent upon the judgement and experience of the glassmaker.

Glasshouse and Furnace

The prosperous glasshouse could afford to build three furnaces, or at least two, in order that the melting, refining and annealing processes might be carried out in separate structures. The small glassmaker worked with one furnace only which served for all three processes. When this was the case the furnace would be constructed on a three-level basis, the lowest compartment serving as a fire chamber, the middle section housing the founding furnace and the top chamber being used for the purpose of annealing. As shown on page 10 the structure was vaulted over, achieving a beehive-like appearance. Such arrangement was quite common during the Middle Ages and later but the ground-plan of the furnace might vary slightly in different regions. Some ovens, such as the northern ones, were circular; others, like those of the Lorrainers who settled in England from the 1560s onward were planned on a square or rectangular system. The openings or 'boccas' varied in size, depending on their location and purpose of usage. An early 15th-century miniature (in the British Museum) illustrating Sir John Mandeville's Travels shows some of the glassworkers in the Jew's hat they were compelled to wear during the Middle Ages, and tends to prove that the glassmaking craft of the ancient Hebrews was still preserved in isolated instances. The furnace illustrated here is circular but appears to have its annealing chamber attached so that the heat flowing from the main furnace was fully utilized.

There is some basis for speculation in the fact that both illustrations show the men working in proximity of the furnace partly bare-footed or bare-toed. Perhaps it is too imaginative to suggest that by such contact with the floor temperature the relative necessary furnace temperature might be tested and the workmen merely considered this a convenient method for warming their feet. Whatever the reason, it seems somewhat mystifying that they should not protect themselves against injuries by glass fragments which must have been lying about on the glasshouse floor.

One of our most informative sources on glassmaking is the work *De re metallica*, libri XII, published in Bâle in 1556 by Georgius Agricola, a doctor and mineralogist active at Chemnitz, Germany. He reports very plainly on the three furnaces: "They cook the material in the first, recook it in the second, and cool it off in the third." We are also indebted to him for the description and illustration of the three-in-one furnace on page 10.

With the passage of time the size of the buildings housing the furnaces increased and by the beginning of the eighteenth century the slightly elliptical, huge chimney cone of the glasshouse became a familiar sight. Factory chimneys had to be tall in order to carry away waste smoke high above the roofs of the city. In 1783 the Irish Parliament passed an act that glasshouse chimneys must have a height of at least 50 ft., and glasshouse cones are known to have been as tall as 150 ft.

The fireproof bricks used for building the furnace are made from infusible clay and cement. In a similar way as cullet is added to a new batch of glass, old disused pots are pulverised and re-used in the making of firebricks. The pots themselves are manufactured from the same clay and, although the choice of a glasshouse site is primarily determined by its fuel and silica supply, its most ideal location is on or near clayey soil. Christopher Merret, translator of *Neri's Art of Glass* (published 1612), states in his notes (1662) that some of the clay for the London glasshouses was sent from Purbeck in the Isle of Wight and adds that Non-such clay mixed with Worcestershire clay made the best and most heat-resistant pots.

Glasshouse pots are always made by hand. Their manufacture is a specialized trade and the pots vary in design and size. A sixteenth-century pot might hold about 400 lb. of molten glass, a nineteenth-century one considerably more—10 or 12 cwt., perhaps. A modern pot may have a capacity of 30 cwt. Pots can be round, oval or rectangular, open or covered and of retort shape for coal-fuelled glasshouses. To achieve the necessary refractory properties the glasshouse pots have to remain in a heating chamber under a constant temperature of 90°–100°F. for a period varying between four and eight months. They will then be tested by exposure to a temperature of 1800° to 2700°F. for an additional period of several weeks. Glass attacks the clay and consequently the pots have to be replaced relatively frequently, normally within two months or so of their original installation. Potsetting—that is to say the removal of a worn pot and the setting of a new one—is the roughest and most hazardous task carried out in the glasshouse. No special pay was awarded to the men, who frequently had to stay on for several hours until the setting was completed, and they were fortunate if they could return home with merely a scorched shirt. Nowadays potsetting is paid work but even with modern factory conditions the task is arduous and may be dangerous.

Tools and Techniques

The techniques of the glass craftsman are as old as Christianity. On page 36 is a reproduction from Haudiquer de Blancourt's book *The Art of Glass*, published in 1699, and shows a set of glassmaker's tools as they were in use during the seventeenth century. The same tools are still in use today. The work of blowing and shaping the plastic glass metal requires toughness and precision and is acquired only with years of practice. From early times the glassmaker's craft has run in families, handed down from father to son, and it is the young apprentice who will eventually make the experienced craftsman. The tools themselves give a fair indication of the work involved. The most indispensable of these is the blowing-iron, a hollow pipe or tube

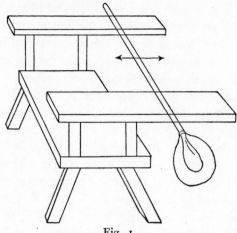

Fig. 1

made of iron with a slightly thickened end for gathering the glass metal, and protected by a wooden covering at points where it is handled. The lump of glass metal, the paraison or parison, is taken from the furnace with the blowpipe or an iron rod, the pontil or pouty. With the pontil glass can be drawn out or twisted, leaving a rough part on the glass surface when it is broken off, the pontil mark. From the collector's point of view some significance is attached to this mark, which will be referred to again later. Instruments such as the rake and the ladle are used for work at the furnace. The shears, large and small, the pincers and the wooden lipper are used during the shaping of the glass object and are hung up on the sides or below the arms of the gaffer's chair. (Fig. 1)

The gaffer is the man in charge, the master glassblower. He is the head of the team, usually consisting of three men and a boy, the footmaker, servitor and apprentice. The gaffer's chair is similar to a short bench with flat and slightly sloping long arms. The term 'chair' not only refers to this particular piece of glasshouse furniture on which the gaffer sits to do most of his work, but also to the whole team of men working together. It is across the long arms of the chair that the gaffer rests his blow pipe and rapidly rolls it backwards and forwards to ensure and maintain a symmetrical shape, or he may roll it smooth on the marver, a polished iron

29

slab. All the work is done with quick precision and in order to maintain the plastic state of the glassmetal it has to be reheated frequently. Larger pieces of glass are sometimes supported during rotation by a semicircular trough or mould of moistened wood, to prevent sagging of the glassbubble and to ensure a perfect shape. By swinging or diverse manipulation of the blow pipe the glass bubble can assume varying shapes. It can be elongated or flattened, it can be shaken in a certain manner to produce a wave pattern or be drawn with the pontil to almost any length. Spun glass is no novel invention; the delicate glass ships (nefs) made in Venice and Liège during the sixteenth century, and the Victorian fanciful birdfountains kept under glass domes as if stuffed, are good examples of the application of spun glass. On the more practical side, R. A. F. de Réaumur (1683–1757), best known for his thermometer, predicted in 1713 that the time would come when "woven stuffs will be made of glass threads".

Prior to the development and adoption of glassblowing during the first Christian era varied techniques were applied to the making of glass in the near Eastern region. Much of this early glass was carved from solid blocks, in the manner of the lapidary or even the stonemason. The stories of enormous emeralds and statues made of this stone most likely refer to blocks of green glass and it may be significant that Herodotus tells of a column of emerald seen at Tyre, one of the cradles of ancient glassmaking.

The casting of glass on stone beds or pressing into hollow moulds were widely practised methods. Small bowls, glass beads and amulets were fashioned in this way, and finds have been made of attractive necklaces of coloured translucent glass, which can be seen in several museums.

It seems likely that large blocks of glass were transported from Egypt and Mesopotamia to glassmakers in adjacent areas, since they had no facilities for producing the raw materials. Such blocks of glass were ground and powdered, making them more easily fusible, and the resultant glass paste could be coldworked. This 'glass-export' theory would account for the similarity of the blue-green translucent glass found over widely scattered areas.

A more complicated but also more interesting method used for making small glass vessels in the near East prior to glassblowing techniques was the cored method of glass-making. Objects fashioned by this process rank amongst the most attractive of glass vessels made in antiquity and fortunately they are abundantly represented in museum collections. As the name implies, this is a method of manufacturing objects made of glass, which is 'built' around a core of perhaps mud and straw. The core is moulded to the desired shape and after being baked a metal rod is inserted. This rod with the core is rotated in the furnace above a crucible of molten glass. With the aid of a second rod, or dipstick, glass is trailed on to the rotating core until it is covered, although small gaps are left to allow for expansion. The coiled glass mass is then marvered smooth and the process repeated until the desired thickness is obtained. By trailing on glass of contrasting colour an attractive decorative effect was achieved which could be heightened by combed or feather patterns. Bright blues and yellows were prevalent colour schemes of this technique and most of the vessels made in this way were small in size, averaging 3 to 4 in. Egyptian furnaces were relatively small; the crucibles for melting the metal were often no more than 2 or 3 in. high.

Blowing into moulds has been practised since the earliest times. The small flasks with ancient Christian and Jewish symbols and the green or bluish-green Roman bottles dating from the first century onward and found so frequently on old Roman glass sites in England, are typical examples of this type of glass treatment. An elaboration of this theme is the extended or expanded mould-blown technique, whereby the glass is in the first instance blown into a mould of certain shape and pattern. After taking the glass from the mould, which can be in two or three parts for easy removal, the glassmaker continues blowing and only a faint suggestion of the original pattern remains. In this way a larger object could be produced from a small mould and still bear traces of decorative effort.

While the interior wall of mould-blown vessels corresponds to the pattern impressed on the outer surface, pressed glass has a smooth interior. For the manufacture of pressed glass a long handled plunger is employed to press the glass mass into the mould. This popular and cheaper method was developed into a highly mechanized process in America and by the middle of the nineteenth century three-quarters of the American glass output consisted of pressed ware.

The making of large panes of glass has always been an ambition of the glass manufacturers. In the previous chapter mention was made of France, and Lucas de Nehou, to whom we are indebted for the invention (1688) of casting and rolling large sheets of glass. Two different methods existed for the manufacture of window glass. Both were used during the same periods, but independently of each other.

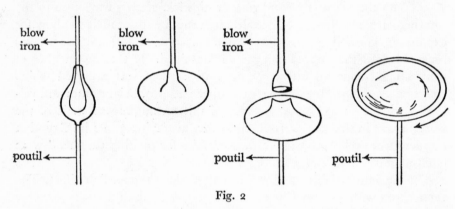

Fig. 2

The crown glass technique (Fig. 2) was dependent upon the dexterity and strength of the gaffer. By this method a bubble of glass was blown and cut open. It was then transferred to the pontil, freely rotated and spun in front of the furnace opening, and frequently reheated. By applying centrifugal force, a large, circular pane of glass was obtained in this way and a very high polish achieved due to repeated reheating, the so-called fire-polish. The finished glass pane was fairly thin and showed the wavy lines caused by the spinning. In the centre of the crown remained the typical bull's eye, the slightly thickened part of the glass to which the pontil, or iron rod, was attached. This part could not be used and was cut out. A nineteenth-century source gives the following composition for crown glass to a pot:

Sand	264 lb.	Chalk	33 lb.
Potash	77 lb.	White arsenic	$2\frac{1}{5}$ lb.
Salt of Soda	44 lb.		

32

Hedwig glass (Islamic) of the 12th century A.D. Wheel-cut in deep relief. Colourless glass with smoky topaz tinge. Ht. 14 cm.

A Syrian mosque lamp (Damascus). Yellowish tinge, enamelled in blue, red, green, yellow and white, with gilding, c. A.D. 1300-40. Ht. 24·7 cm.

Venetian standing cup and cover of the second half of the 15th century. Wrythen gilt ribs ornament on bowl and cover, the borders enamelled in white, blue, red and with gilding. Ht. 42·1 cm.

An English soda-glass goblet engraved with diamond point, from Verzelini's glasshouse. Inscribed 1578 and with initials 'A.T.' and 'R.T.' Ht. 21·5 cm.

The method of manufacturing window glass by the crown process is generally regarded as the Normandy method, because its introduction into England is attributed to the Norman glassmakers. However, the method was in use long before they arrived on our shores and it may well have been brought to the West by Syrian immigrant gaffers.

The wastage caused by cutting straight pieces of glass from circular panels, and by removal of the bull's eye, is avoided in the manufacture of window glass by the broadsheet technique (Fig. 3), practised by the

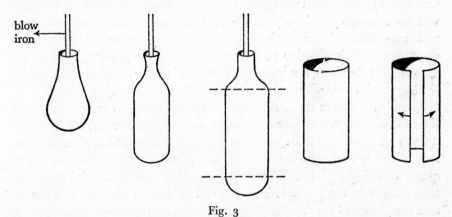

blow iron

Fig. 3

Lorrainer glassmakers and described in Theophilus' treatise as early as 1100. Broadsheet is manufactured by blowing and swinging the paraison in such a way as to form a long cylinder, which is opened and cut off straight at both ends. The resultant cylinder is placed on to a wooden stand and cut open lengthwise by passing a hot iron straight down the inside. The opened cylinder is then placed into a 'flattening oven' where it is re-heated and flattened by passing a wooden plane over the glass and finally using the polissoir, a wooden tool which makes the sheet a perfect plane. Today, of course, the manufacture of sheet glass is entirely mechanized and runs as a continuous process. Float glass, one of the most advanced methods of producing plate glass, was invented and developed by the British firm of Pilkington Brothers and is earning millions of pounds in sales and royalties from other countries.

c

33

The stability and durability of glass is dependent on its composition and subsequent treatment. Glass can be attacked by various 'diseases', the most common being that of crystallization or even devitrification. (Deliberately crystallized glass, so called 'sitals', is used for high-temperature applications.) If glass is heated above its hot working temperature it will become liquid, and at a certain temperature known as the devitrification temperature it will remain in a liquid state without any changes occurring. If, however, the metal is kept below the devitrification temperature for a certain length of time it devitrifies or crystallizes, i.e., it forms crystals and will have a milky-white appearance. The watery, milky alabasters, in which the white cloudiness is formed by a mass of crystallized silica, are examples of devitrification purposely introduced. Many such defects are known only to the glass worker. They make the metal unsuitable for working and a new glass batch will be used.

Crizzling is one of the defects that may come to light only after a long time lapse. The disease commences at the glass surface, which is always damp and gives off a faint, sour smell. Apart from too high an alkali content, a further reason for crizzling of early glass might have been an inadequacy of firing and the difficulty of reaching and maintaining a high temperature in the furnace. There is still no known cure for this disease and the glass will eventually disintegrate despite treatment by lacquer or by vacuum.

A defect frequently found in lead glasses of the Baroque period is the presence of small, porous sulphate stones which form a whitish bloom. This is the residue of lead sulphate which has not dissolved during melting and has been formed by the lead and the potassium sulphate contained in the potash. In this connection an interesting suggestion has been made by Dr. M. B. Volf in his book *Sklo* (Glass), Prague, 1947. In his opinion the dense network of delicate criss-cross lines, applied in matcut on some early glasses, was the glass cutter's camouflage of areas showing such defects.

The highest proportioned ingredient in glass manufacture is silica. Some of Ravenscroft's glasses have the astonishingly high silica content of 88%. Iron, which is present in sand, the glassmaker's main source of silica, and in plant ash, will produce a metal of greenish tinge. Other impurities may impart a yellow or different colour. To obtain a glass free from colour a variety of substances may be added, the most common being 'glassmaker's soap' (manganese dioxide). When added to the glass batch, manganese dioxide will bring about the change of ferrous silicate to ferric silicate, which is a pale shade of green. The amethyst pink produced by the manganese silicate will neutralize this green colouring and a colourless metal is the result. The art of producing a colourless glass had been lost for some centuries and it fell to the Venetians to develop a clear, sparkling glass. The Venetian glassmaker's ambition was to produce a metal akin to the natural rock crystal and he called his new glass 'cristallo'. Nevertheless, even cristallo glass was not entirely free from impurities and in consequence had to be blown fairly thin to avoid the slight greyish or brownish tinge often noticeable in soda glass.

The green or reddish-yellow colour common to bottle glass was produced by additional quantities of iron in the form of iron oxide. When tin-oxide is substituted the resultant glassy substance is enamel. The addition of lead-oxide (red minium) to the metal led to the development of crystal or lead glass.

A word might be said here regarding the term flint-glass. This always signifies glass of lead and possibly one of the reasons for use of this term were the ground flintstones, in fact the blackest flintstones which are most free from iron, used by Ravenscroft during the development of his lead glass. Dr. Ludwell of Wadham College, Oxford, made an analysis of Ravenscroft's early glass metal and stated: "to a pound of the blackest flints calcined and white christalline sand, about two ounces of Nitre, Tartar and Borax." This does not seem very explicit but we cannot really blame Ravenscroft for being a little cagey about his glass composition, particularly at this early stage. The 'christalline' sand mentioned was obviously the source of silica, as was also most probably the black flint. Nitre, which nowadays signifies potassium nitrate or saltpetre, was in Ravenscroft's day the term used for sodium carbonate or soda; hence the mistaken belief that all Ravenscroft's early glass was potash glass.

Before concluding this chapter one particular glass disease must be mentioned which, far from being considered a blemish, constitutes one of the most eagerly sought-after phenomena for the ambitious glass collector. This is the 'weathering' to which ancient glass is subjected and which may result in a most attractive, lustrous patina, the iridescence. Iridescence is caused by long exposure to damp earth or air and results in a scintillating film of rainbow colours on the surface of the glass. During the progressive stage of this disease the glass surface becomes scaly and flakes off, and with increasing iridescence the object becomes lighter. Weathering iridescence bears no relation to the iridescent lustre of some early glass which is produced for decorative effect and obtained by admixture, or a film, of metallic oxides. On the contrary, it appears that opaque glass embellished in this way is rarely susceptible to irisation, while transparent glass that has been treated by a decolourizing agent will show the most brilliant iridescence. Weathering affects only the glass surface; there is no danger of eventual disintegration of the object, although where the glass is very thin there is obviously high fragility.

Irisation of glass produces a strikingly decorative effect, brought about entirely by the action of nature. The question must now be considered of how the artist deals with the problem of ornamental treatment of glass and the means which are at his disposal.

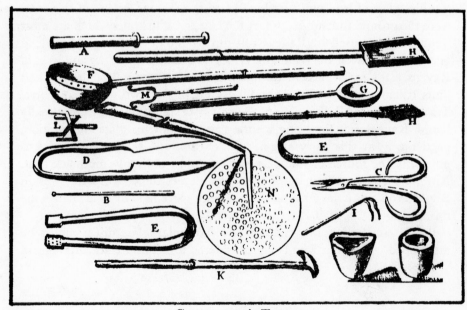

GLASS-MAKER'S TOOLS
Engraving from Haudicquer de Blancourt's *The Art of Glass,* 1699

3
Glassmaking as Artistic Inspiration

Glass is a transparent, refractive material. Due to its malleability, strength and beauty, and the comparatively simple means by which it can be manufactured, it holds a unique position in the history of man-made materials. It can be used for replacing a variety of media, natural and artificial, from imitation jewellery to building bricks and draperies.

Light and colour are prominent factors in the decorative effects of glass and if we reflect once more upon its method of manufacture we find that the ornamental treatment of glass falls into two distinct categories. In the first instance, ornamental effects are achieved by exploiting the ductility of the liquid metal to its fullest extent. Artistic appeal relies on the ability and inspiration of the gaffer and the design is complete before the object reaches the annealing oven. To the second category belongs the problem of embellishing the already finished 'cold' glass. This is done away from the furnace, by an artisan specialized in a particular field of glass decoration. Such glass artists might be creative in other media as well; Anna Roemers Visscher (1583–1651) and David Wolff (1723–98), for example, were traditionally painters, even though to the glass collector they are the exponents of Dutch glass engraving.

These two distinct approaches to embellishment have produced artistic glass of infinite variety and ingenuity. When the two methods are sympathetically mated we obtain a truly perfect piece of glass. This was achieved in particular by the French glass artists of the Art Nouveau period. Here, artist-designer turned gaffer and inspiration was expressed by the medium of glass and echoed or supplemented in the applied decoration.

The early gaffer was not lacking in enterprise when exploring the possibilities of his medium. He could shape his glass at will, press it, blow it free or into a pre-designed mould and draw or twist the flexible metal with the pontil. He used his pincers to make ribbed or pinched decorations such as the 'Nipped Diamond Waies' (NDW), or applied threads or blobs of glass as shown on the claw beakers. Both treatments were popular with the Seine–Rhine glassmakers during the fifth century and later.

Colour

The problem of colouring glass has presented a fascinating challenge to glassmakers from antiquity to the present day. By admixture of certain metallic oxides an almost unlimited range of colour has been produced.

Until the discovery of decolourizing agents such as manganese dioxide (glassmaker's soap), colouring of glass was accidental. The deliberate colouring was a natural result of the realization that sand from different areas would produce a different colour effect in the glass metal. The earliest coloured glass was opaque. Blues and greens were achieved by the grinding down and addition to the glass paste of green and blue stones, such as malachite and lapis lazuli. Addition of manganese would produce a violet-pink shade, and the browns and greens of modern bottle glass are the result of additions of iron ore. Copper and Cobalt were available to early glassmakers and in their various compounds are used to produce both green and blue colouring. The introduction of cuprous oxide particles into the glass mass resulted in the famous Alexandrian Heamatite or blood-glass, but the ruby glass developed about 1680 by Johann Kunckel at Potsdam was obtained by the admixture of gold. Copper oxide is used for green and red, chromium oxide for yellow and green colouring. Bone ash, antimony and tin oxide in particular, produce a white, opaque glass, such as for instance the attractive Bristol milk-glass, which formed so perfect a background for the enamels of Michael Edkins, the most famous of Bristol glass-painters (during the years 1760–80). Opaque white glass (It. Lattimo) is also loosely termed 'enamel' glass, particularly when referring to Bristol manufacture. Opaque white glass was manufactured by diverse glass-houses but that ascribed to Bristol is of a particularly smooth and solid white colour, almost unidentifiable from porcelain at a cursory glance.

Metallic flakes of copper and gold were often introduced and attractively manipulated in the glass mass. The Venetian 'Aventurine' glass, a clear glass enclosing flakes of copper, gained its name from the accidental addition of metallic flakes. The contrasting colour streaks of the Alexandrian and Roman 'murrhine' bowls and the mosaic and millefiori glass produced during the first few centuries A.D., testify to the craftsmanship and artistic ingenuity of the early glassmakers. The manufacture of a coloured opaque glass mass by introducing coloured ground stones was a relatively simple process. The colouring of transparent glass, however, presented a far greater problem. The colouring agent had to go into the melting pot and the reactions and changes that occur in the furnace necessitated a good deal of experimental testing before this art was perfected. With the solution to such problems successfully accomplished, the gaffer's ingenuity produced results of astonishing nuance and dexterity.

The method of making mosaic glass was developed by Alexandrian glassmakers about the second or first centuries B.C. It was produced by arranging coloured glass pieces of varied shape on a clay base and heated in a furnace. In this way the edges of the mosaics were fused together and the resultant mosaic glass plaques made ductile by re-heating. They could then be shaped into bowls or vessels and finished by grinding.

The term *millefiori* (literally, thousands of flowers), as applied to glass, originated in renaissance Venice but the technique of making millefiori glass is very much older and was developed by Egyptian glassmakers about the fifteenth or fourteenth centuries B.C. In certain variations millefiori glass may bear a resemblance to mosaic glass but it is produced by an entirely different and much more complicated method, which has an astonishingly far reaching effect.

The inventive glassmakers developed several variations of millefiori glass, all of them relying on the ductility of the glass metal which can be drawn to infinite length. Basically the technique consists of arranging glass canes of different colours into bundles in such a way that their cross-section would show an attractive pattern. When the bundle was heated it could be drawn thin and the pattern of the cross-section would be perfectly miniaturized.

We need only imagine sticks of seaside rock or those tiny, round sweets with a multicolour flower pattern in the centre, which might be sucked smaller and smaller yet still keep their pattern. The coloured glass rods were encased in glass of any chosen colour, sometimes transparent white, sometimes of strong contrasting colour. The expression 'true' millefiori glass refers to bundles which show a star pattern in cross-section. This was achieved by marvering the flexible glass rod on a grooved surface and the indentation at regular intervals would press the pattern into its star shape. Vessels of millefiori glass are produced by the same method as is applied to mosaic work. The finished drawn canes are sliced up and the pieces placed side by side on a clay tablet and fused together to be hot-shaped into the desired object.

An elaborated technique of this method are the millefiori paper-weights and inkbottles fashionable during the first half of the nineteenth century and perfected in French glasshouses, notably Baccarat and Clichy. These objects have become desirable collector's items but they are not particularly difficult to manufacture and modern reproductions are abundant. A portion of millefiori glass, usually of particularly colourful pattern is encased between two layers of clear glass and domed over by a further layer so that a hemispherical shape is obtained. This can be achieved by means of a concave spatula of moistened wood, with the result that the domed glass mass acts as a magnifying lens. The optical illusion of flowers growing out of the crystal is most successfully created in this way. Care must be taken that no air bubble remains trapped in the surrounding glass mass to spoil the crystal clarity of the metal (plate facing p. 97).

French glassmakers were also among the first to experiment with *cristallo-ceramie*, a process of ornamental cameo incrustation attempted about 1750 in Bohemia. The name of an Englishman, Apsley Pellatt, will always be linked with this type of glass ornamentation. Apsley Pellatt, born in 1791, came from a long line of Apsley Pellatts, although Thorpe names him as Apsley Pellatt II, since his father Apsley Pellatt was the founder of the firm which took over the Falcon Glass Works in Southwark about 1790. After returning from a journey to France, Pellatt began to perfect the process of cameo incrustation and in 1820 obtained a patent of fourteen years dura-

Persian rose-water sprinkler of the typical blue colour associated
with Shiraz, late 18th century. Ht. 17 cm.

tion. His process consisted of a refractory material, such as white china clay and a supersilicate of potash which fuses at a much higher temperature than glass, being moulded into medallions or shaped reliefs and enclosed in a transparent glass mass. This was accomplished by pushing the finished cameo into a hollow blown bulb which was cut open at the end for this purpose. The air in the glass bulb was sucked back by the gaffer so that the surrounding glass mass would adhere closely to the incrustation. Cameo incrustations of small size could be heated and applied to the hot glass surface and covered by a layer of transparent glass. Incrustations of this type are also called 'sulphides', or 'sulfures' in French glass (plate facing p. 113).

Coloured glass windows were already known in the sixth century. The glass from which they were made was coloured through by addition of metal oxides to the glass batch, the coloured mass then being described as 'pot metal'.

The glass for stained windows was treated in an entirely different way and the invention of staining glass most likely dates only as far back as the fourteenth century. Up to the beginning of the fourteenth century no method was known of suitably colouring the glass surface, with the exception of a brownish-black pigment which would fuse with the glass surface when heated in a kiln. By the revolutionary oxidation process of staining glass, silver nitrate was applied to the glass surface and after heating in the furnace a lovely yellow colour of varying tone was obtained, the 'yellow stain'. A red pot metal was difficult to utilize since this colour proved too dense to possess the necessary transparency for window glass. Mediaeval glaziers solved this problem by coating white glass with a thin layer of copper-ruby glass, a process known as 'flashing'. It is worthwhile to mention here that ultramarine blue was not developed until the beginning of the nineteenth century and production commenced in England in 1826. The warmth and variance of tone of ultramarine blue is far removed from the cool, clear blues to be found, for instance, in northern mediaeval stained glass.

During the Renaissance, when oil-painting became a practised art, windows too were figuratively decorated by applying oil-colours. A piece of glass would be treated as if it were canvas, and the late Canon Harrison says in his notes on the stained glass of York Minster: "Glass ceased to be a window and became only a picture. The jewel-like effect of the sun's rays shining through myriads of tiny pieces of brilliantly coloured and mostly unpainted glass was thought not to be worth striving after."

No coloured glass was made in England during the Middle Ages. It was imported from the Continent, specifically from Germany and France. In 1449 Henry IV granted a twenty-year monopoly for making coloured glass to a Flemish glassmaker, John of Utynam, but nothing is known of his product and coloured glass continued to be a foreign import. Although the Lorrainers were conversant with the techniques of colouring glass, they do not appear to have applied this particular knowledge after their arrival on English shores.

The technique of embedding contrasting coloured glass canes in the glass mass found its greatest response in the *latticinio* glass. This consisted of the ingenious application of opaque white glass threads to clear transparent glass and was developed by the sixteenth-century Venetian gaffers. The designs and patterns of latticinio glass depend on the manipulation and twist of the individual filigree canes and accordingly it is also named vitro-di-trina, filigree glass or lace- (German: netz-) glass, or reticello.

The method of developing twisted filigree canes was applied to that most collectable of English drinking glasses, the opaque white twist or enamel twist, popular during the years 1745 to about 1780. To produce such canes with spiral threads the interior of a cylindrical mould of pottery or metal is lined with canes of opaque white glass alternating with rods of transparent colourless glass. For stems of English opaque white twists the colourless glass canes are of identical size to the coloured canes. The cylindrical container is heated to a temperature a little below red heat, at which it is safe to fill the empty space in the centre with a mass of molten colourless glass. The glass rods adhere to the central glass mass and the whole mass is drawn out by the workman with his pincers in one hand while with the iron rod in the other he twists and manipulates the glass thread until the desired thickness and effect is obtained. In principle, Italian sixteenth-century methods and eighteenth-century English techniques for the manufacture of twisted glass canes were similar, with the only difference that the Murano workmen reheated the whole mass in the cylindrical mould, cut off one end of the mould and drew and twisted the glass directly from its container. This seems a more practical method but allows less freedom to the workman for manipulating his material. For producing a latticinio ornamentation, rods of filigree glass were symmetrically arranged around the inside of a cylindrical mould into which a colourless, transparent glass bubble was blown. The canes adhere to this glass bubble and by continuous blowing and twisting the paraison would be covered by a spiral network of filigree. As soon as the gaffer withdrew the paraison from the mould an assistant covered the filigree network with a band of soft transparent glass, so that the canes would be firmly embedded in the glass surface. After reheating and marvering, the glass cylinder was pinched together at its extremity so that all the canes were united at a central point. At this stage the glass was ready to receive its final shape, which was achieved by further blowing and twisting. To obtain a true lace or netzglas effect the gaffer sucked one half of the glass bulb back into the other and the opaque colour trails would cross each other to form a symmetrical network. Another method by which this effect could be achieved was to blow one glassbubble inside another with contrary spiralling opaque trails. An exceptionally attractive feature of some netzglas is provided by small silvery air bubbles which have become trapped in the square spaces of the mesh formed (plate facing p. 64).

A trapped air bubble is also considered to have been the inspiration of that very English glass technique, the 'air-twist', a form of decoration applied to stems of English drinking-glasses and prevalent during the second quarter of the eighteenth century. It is generally accepted that air-twists originated with the air bubble or 'tear', often imprisoned at the base of the bowl or the upper part of baluster stems, and that they are merely elongated 'tears'. These bubbles or tears, which may originally have been accidental, were made by pricking the hot glass with a tool and covering the hollow or hollows thus formed with a layer of melted glass. The imprisoned air bubbles could be drawn out and twisted at will, but the making of air-twist stems required greater skill and was based on a technically more elaborate process. In the method employed, a cylindrical mould with an interior grooved or fluted surface was filled with a mass of glass. When the glass was withdrawn from the mould its surface was ridged or fluted. The glass cylinder was then surrounded by a mass of hot glass and sealed at the ends, so that the hollows between the ridges were filled with trapped air. The glass rods obtained by this method were drawn out and twisted much in the manner of enamel twists. Early air-twist glasses were made in two parts, the stem being drawn from the bowl, which was generally funnel- or trumpet-shaped, and the foot welded on to the stem. With the development of the three-piece technique, where foot, stem and bowl were made as separate units and then welded together, a greater variety was achieved in bowl and stem design of air-twist glasses. The variety of twist was dependent upon the skill of the workman. The somewhat misleading term 'mercury twist' refers to air-twists of particularly brilliant reflection which is the result of a broad but closely twisted spiral. An ingenious variety of twist combination was produced during the eighteenth century, and these will be referred to later.

Ice-glass or crackle-glass was a surface embellishment developed in Venice during the sixteenth century. As its name implies, this decorative surface effect resembles cracked ice in appearance and could be achieved in two ways, both relatively simple. By the first method the hot glass bulb was quenched in water for a moment and consequently reheated and blown fully to the required size. The quenching caused a labyrinth of fissures which covered the glass surface. A similar effect was achieved by rolling the soft glass bubble on the iron table (marver), covered for this purpose with powdered glass fragments. These glass chips adhered to the soft surface of the glass bulb with which they fused during reheating. Further blowing obliterated the sharp edges. The latter method was frequently employed by nineteenth-century French glass manufacturers and known as '*Brocs à glaces*'. (Pl. between pp. 72–73.)

Glass has been employed for imitation precious stones since antiquity. A delightful story exists of Salonina, wife of the Roman emperor Gallienus who reigned from A.D. 260 to 268. The empress had purchased some jewels which proved to be made of glass and she demanded of the emperor that the jeweller be thrown to the lions in the circus. The unhappy victim prepared himself to die, watched by thousands of spectators. When the animal's cage was opened, a cockerel strutted out, crowing loudly. The emperor had decided that this was sufficiently just punishment.

Schmelzglas, developed by the Venetians about the same time as their latticinio glass, is a coloured opaque glass composition designed to imitate marble and similar semi-precious stones, such as the agates and chalcedony. The most successful revival of this form of glass effect is achieved in the 'Lithyalin' glass developed in Bohemia by Friedrich (Bedrich) Egermann (1777–1864), and exhibited for the first time in Prague in 1829.

The inventiveness of the gaffer, and the possibilities available to him for exploiting the plastic properties of his material, appear unlimited, His task ends with the emergence of the finished object from the annealing chamber. At this point, any desired embellishment is entrusted to the hands of someone outside the gaffer's immediate surroundings—the glass artist.

Basically, two distinct courses lay open to the imaginative artist and both had been pursued successfully for centuries. He could add to visual enjoyment by decorating his object with jewel-like enamels, or he could satisfy more aesthetic tastes by making the best possible use of the refractive and lapidary properties of his material.

The most perfect examples of enamelling were produced in the Islamic style during its great period of flourishing, from A.D. 1250 to 1400, at the main centres of Raqqa, Aleppo and Damascus. The 'Luck of Edenhall' beaker is a celebrated example of Saracen enamelled and gilded glass. It was made as early as the middle or end of the thirteenth century and was not, as the story tells, snatched by the family butler from fairies at the well, but had most likely been brought to England by an early Crusader as a souvenir of a colourful episode of history (Victoria and Albert Museum).

Enamel paints are made from a glass composition base with a fluxing additive, often borax, to facilitate melting which must take place at a lower temperature than glass. Enamel paints were often laid over an opaque white or gilt base. A higher brilliancy of colour was obtained by this method, particularly useful when the glass itself was coloured, as for instance the cobalt blue glass of Renaissance Venice and France. Prior application of a gilt base would create the appearance of an enamelled design faintly outlined in gold. In order to make the paint adhere permanently to the glass surface, it was necessary to place the enamelled object in a specially constructed furnace or kiln, the 'muffle kiln', where the colours could be fired and then gradually cooled before annealing.

Gilding—the use of gold or gold leaf for painting glass—was known in antiquity, and to render this type of decoration permanent it, too, had to be fired after application to the glass.

Both enamelling and gilding could and were, applied by the cold technique—the German *Kaltmalerei*. The large German Humpen made of forest glass (German *Waldglas*), were usually decorated by this technique, partly because many such vessels were too large to be conveniently fired in a muffle kiln and partly because the glass was not of sufficiently good quality to withstand renewed firing. A further reason is that much of this particular type of enamelling was a rustic craft—carried out by the peasant artisan of the mountain and forest regions, who simply did not have access to a furnace.

The technique of painting in thin, transparent enamels was developed, with delightful results, by the two Mohns—father (1762–1815) and son (1789–1825)—who worked in Dresden during the early nineteenth century.

The application of gold on glass, without firing, was achieved by means of oil-gilding and was practised mainly during the eighteenth century. Continental oil-gilding, particularly Bohemian and German, seems to have lasted better than that carried out in England, due to some particularly effective cement which was employed as adhesive. Rubbed-away oil-gilding can usually be detected on the glass in the form of a fine film (the remnant adhesive) and the original pattern of the gilding can be traced by this.

Kaltmalerei was not as lasting as fired enamelling and it can be scraped off with a knife. Repaired enamelling may normally be detected in this way. By the end of the sixteenth century the jewel-like Venetian enamelling had passed its zenith, but Venetian enamel colours continued to be considered superior and were exported all over Europe in the form of small cakes.

In the early Christian era a particular technique was in use for protecting gold paintings on glass. This is the *Zwischengold* (literally from the

German 'in-between-gold') method. A piece of glass was decorated on its reverse side and the embellished part was covered with a further layer of transparent colourless glass, so that the gold decoration was 'sandwiched' in between. This particular technique was revived and greatly perfected by Bohemian glass artists during the first half of the eighteenth century and Kunckel mentions this method a little earlier in his *Ars vitraria experimentalis* (1687). The Bohemian Zwischengold glass usually takes the form of 12- to 18-faceted beakers consisting of two vessels, one fitting perfectly into the other. The decoration is a design etched with a needle on gold leaf applied to the inner beaker, and sometimes augmented by silverfoil and colour. A colourless resin between the two walls served as adhesive. The great difficulty was to exclude any air bubbles which might easily become entrapped between the two glass layers. The joint of eighteenth-century Zwischengold glasses was situated on the outside, about 1 cm. below the rim of the beaker. The rim of the inner beaker was of double thickness to 1 cm. down, forming a lip that fitted and joined perfectly when placed into the outer beaker. The base of Zwischengold glass is similarly treated and decorated; it is removed from the outer vessel and after decoration a disc of glass is cut to fit perfectly into the void. The earliest Zwischengold glass made in Bohemia shows the joint at the top of the rim. It differs in decorative design and is exceedingly rare. (See p. 86.)

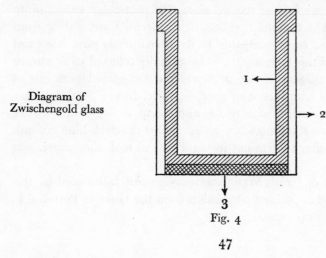

Diagram of
Zwischengold glass

Fig. 4

The embellishment of glass by cutting is a step in an entirely different direction. The most outstanding achievements in this art are the 'dietrata' or cage-cups, superb pieces of glass craft datable to the first three centuries A.D. They are ovoid-shaped cups, some of them about 12 cm. high, and consist of an outer layer in the form of an intricate trellis work cut away from the wall of the vessel, but still attached to it by small struts which often terminate in some embellished form. The letters, which usually encircle the cup below the rim, are undercut in the same way from the main body of the vessel which is made of transparent colourless glass. The net- or cage-work and the lettering in most existing examples is of coloured glass. Dietrata are supreme proof of the artist's complete mastery over the fragility of his material and we can only speculate how this was achieved. Although the majority of cage-cups have been found in the Rhineland, the workmanship is more congenial to the spirit of the East and is attributed to Roman workmen who had been influenced by the assimilation of the Eastern people during Roman occupation. Glass is a material of great vulnerability and the placidity and patience required for the carving of dietrata is a natural asset of the oriental attitude of mind. If these cage-cups were indeed cut from one single thick-walled vessel, and it seems that this is so, the transparent, colourless glass body must have been flashed by a coloured glass mass which was then undercut.

The technique of overlaid or flashed glass is of particular attraction to the creative artist. The famous Portland or Barberini Vase, dating from the first century A.D., represents, due to its adventurous past, the most notorious example of this technique and is normally referred to as 'cameo glass'. Cameo glass consists of two or more coloured glass layers, one of these usually being a translucent or opaque white. In the Portland Vase the deep blue base is flashed with white, and the mythological motifs are exquisitely carved in a startling white relief against the dark-blue ground. The technique is similar to gem cutting and a hand tool, the graver, was employed.

The pottery work of Josiah Wedgwood was greatly influenced by this cameo-like effect and he gained permission from the Duke of Portland to copy the vase in his jasperware.

Above, mid-17th-century covered goblet from the Netherlands. Colourless glass, diamond-engraved with inscriptions and calligraphic flourishes, presumably by Willem van Heemskerk. Ht. 36·5 cm. ; *left*, a Netherlands Flügelglas, 'façon de Venise', of the second half of the 17th century. Red, white and blue spiral serpentine stem with blue pincered wings. Ht. 26·7 cm.

English lead-glass posset-pot with vertical mould-blown ribbing. From George Ravenscroft's Savoy glasshouse, it has a raven's head seal at the base of the spout; *c.* 1677–8. Ht. 9·5 cm.

Venetian goblets of the late 17th or early 18th century: *left*, decoration consists of broad spirals in white latticinio. Ht. 13·3 cm.; *right*, white latticinio decoration. Ht. 14 cm.

During the later half of the nineteenth century a great revival of cameo glass art sprang up on the Continent and in England. A remarkable feature of this vogue in glass was the fact that with similarly applied techniques the glass-making countries involved developed individually characteristic styles that bore little resemblance to each other. While George Woodall made cameo glass for the Stourbridge workshop of Thomas Webb, Emile Gallé designed his cased glass vessels and created the 'Ecole de Nancy'. Both men used the process of cameo glass as a means for artistic expression. It is unlikely that even the most inexperienced collector would confuse their work.

Cutting and engraving of glass has always been most successfully accomplished in countries with old traditions of the lapidary's art. Lathe cutting and some beautifully executed engraving can be found on Roman vessels of the first century A.D. Later examples of wheel cutting are the Hedwig glasses, so called because one of these surviving glass beakers supposedly belonged to St. Hedwig, the patron saint of Silesia who died in A.D. 1243. Hedwig glasses are thick-walled and deeply cut in high relief. The pattern is highly stylized and almost geometrical, even when the design is figurative. Little is known of their origin but they are thought to have been developed in Egypt, or Byzantium, perhaps about A.D. 1100. The abrasive techniques of glass-cutting by means of the copper wheel as practised in these glasses seems to have been lost in occidental countries during mediaeval times. It is possible that the great influence of glass *à la façon de Venise* was partly responsible for the temporary suppression of the art of cutting. Venetian glass was exported throughout Europe and the thinness of the metal made it unsuitable for cutting or engraving at the wheel. The great innovator of glass engraving, Caspar Lehmann (1570–1622) of Prague, applied his lapidary technique to glass prior to the perfection of a more durable lead crystal. In 1609 Caspar Lehmann, who held the post of royal lapidary to Rudolf II, was invested with a title and granted a monopoly for his technique of glass engraving.

Cutting and engraving as it had been applied to the natural rock crystal became possible with the development of a more suitable glass metal, the lead or flint glass. The apparatus used for cutting glass is as old as the lapidary's craft. Turning of the wheel was facilitated by using the treadle, an innovation attributed to Lehmann. Three or four exchangeable wheels are used in succession for the cutting of glass. The first wheel is made of iron and used for rough cutting. The sand, which is moistened by means of a wooden (water) trough placed above the wheel, is thrown on to it by a workman. The second wheel, of sandstone, continues the cutting process and is replaced by a third, made of wood, on to which pulverized sand is trickled from time to time. Emery and putty powder are also used for the final polishing process, which is completed by application of dry tin putty or the use of a cork wheel. Since the process is laborious and costly, glass is often part-moulded and then brought to the wheel for finished cutting and polishing. A large percentage of modern imported cut glass is treated in this way, particularly when the object is large and heavy.

The basic apparatus for engraving glass is similar to that used for cutting but the wheel is replaced by a spindle terminating in a tempered steel or flint point, against which the glass is pressed when following the lightly traced design. For shallow engraving a tiny copper wheel replaces the spindle's terminal point. Thin-walled vessels are not suitable for spindle or wheel engraving; they may crack on actual contact or through vibration of the rotating spindle, and are, therefore, engraved by hand with a diamond point.

In accordance with the usage and the type of wheel employed, and the added skill of the cutter or engraver, a variety of effects can be achieved. The engraving may be coarse or delicate and the design applied in high or low relief, similar to the techniques of cameo and intaglio cutting.

One of the finest techniques in surface decoration was excelled in by eighteenth-century Dutch engravers. Their superb diamond stippling was a method by which portraits or allegorical pictures were engraved by thousands of minute dots and dashes executed with a diamond point or a steel needle embedded in a hammer. Some of the best work in this technique was produced during the years 1780–95 by David Wolff (plate facing p. 96).

Etching of glass by means of hydrofluoric acid has a somewhat uncertain history. Heinrich Schwanhardt of Bohemia used a medium named 'aqua fortis' for etching glass in about 1670 and he may unwittingly have been the discoverer of hydrofluoric acid. The chemical discovery of hydrofluoric acid was made by Scheele of Sweden in 1771, but acid etching cannot be said to have come into use until the mid-nineteenth century. Glass decor- ated in this way is first coated with a varnish of wax and turpentine applied hot by means of a brush. A varnish of drying linseed oil has the added advantage that its transparency allows easier tracing of the pattern or design outlined on the glass surface. The design is traced with a pointed tool so that the glass surface is laid bare where required. The parts covered with varnish are finally coated with wax and the acid is allowed to eat into the glass. The depth of engraving depends entirely upon the length of time the acid is permitted to remain on the glass. Water and diluted alcohol are employed for removal of the varnish. The characteristic action of acid biting into glass makes it easily distinguishable from glass etched by mechanical means, due to the slight roughness of outline which can always be detected, particularly when a magnifying glass is used. The attractive 'satin' ware of the late nineteenth century was achieved by the acid method applied in reverse. The decorative design was protected against the action of acid which covered the remainder of the entire sur- face and produced a glass which had the feel and look of satin.

It may be argued that the mechanical treatment known as sandblasting is the most modern innovation in glass decoration. In fact sandblasting is no more than a technical variant of the abrasive technique of sand driven by the wheel, and hydrofluoric acid must be considered the only modern addition to the media available to the glassmaker since antiquity.

4
Glassmaking Countries through the Ages

Ancient Glass and the Near East

Pliny's colourful account of the origin of glass, written in A.D. 30, tells of Phoenician traders who had landed on the coast of Palestine and utilized cases of their cargo of natron on which to place their cooking pots, since no stones could be found in the sandy region near the River Belus with which to build a cooking hearth. The action of fire on the natron blocks caused the alkali to form a flux for the sand and the liquid produced proved to be a glassy substance. Whether scientific knowledge supports this theory or not, the story serves to emphasize the belief of the near Eastern Mediterranean as the cradle of glassmaking, and it accentuates the trading activities of the Phoenician seafarers, who extended their commercial enterprise to include areas as distant as Moravia and Scandinavia.

The Phoenicians themselves have left no traces that might indicate the existence of a national art. They were adaptable craftsmen but in artistic design relied entirely on the models of near neighbours. Until about the fourth century B.C. artistic influence was confined to Egypt and, to a limited extent, to Asiatic sources. After the annexation by Alexander's forces the Hellenistic influence became predominant.

So-called Phoenician (Sidonian or Phoenician-Assyrian) glass is a replica of work done in Egypt and the Alexandrian workshops; cored vessels for instance are quite indistinguishable from their Egyptian counterparts. 'Aggry' beads are often attributed to Phoenician manufacture; their dispersal over such widely separated and distant areas certainly points to distribution by a seafaring nation. They are tubular beads of coloured glass layers shaped off at both ends by facet-cutting which reveals the coloured sections in a zigzag pattern. Almost all techniques of glass-making have been applied to beads, pendants and amulets and are consistent with the methods prevalent at the time of manufacture. (For further study see Frederick Neuburg's *Glass in Antiquity*, London, 1949). (Plate facing p. 17.)

Egypt and Alexandria

The earliest glass vessels have been found in Egypt. From finds in royal tombs we know of multicoloured glass paste and enamel inlays, and cored vessels appeared in Egypt about 1500 B.C. They were produced by what is still known as the sandcore technique, although recent research seems to indicate that perhaps other materials were used, not sand. Early cored vessels are often of amusing shape with attractive combed decoration and many interesting finds relating to this period were made during the excavations at Tel-El-Amarna in 1891–3, directed by Sir Flinders Petrie. Tel-El-Amarna is the site of the deserted city of Khuenaten founded by Amenhotep IV (1383–1365 B.C.). Amenhotep left the capital of Thebes shortly after his succession, established a new city, a new fashion of dress and adopted the worship of Aten, in whose honour he changed his name to Akhenaten. The artistic style of this period reflects a realistic influence, possibly due to the Syrian princess who became Akhenaten's queen bringing with her Syrian culture and Syrian craftsmen. The naturalistic, flowing style of the flower and plant forms which decorate excavated buildings differs distinctly from the stylistic conception of contemporary Egyptian art. By 1100 B.C. the Egyptian glassmakers seem to have lost a good deal of their ingenuity, and cored vessels ceased to be made. They reappear, however, around 600 B.C. and most of the surviving objects date from this later period (plate facing p. 17).

Cored vessels are relatively small, averaging between 3 to 5 in. Larger pieces such as a 7-in. alabastron at the Museum of Toledo (Ohio) are somewhat of an exception. These small and often attractive vessels were used as 'unguentaria'—receptacles for ointments, perfumes and kohl and the glass sticks used for their application are occasionally found inside, still intact. Many of these glass containers have a rounded or pointed base without foot and rest on special stands made of glass or even gold. Cored glass objects are either fire-polished or ground smooth. The vessels of the later period can be divided into four main groups. The plainest of these is the 'alabastron', a cylindrical container with a rounded base and flat-rimmed orifice. A pair of minute, looped handles is usually applied to the upper part of the body, their only conceivable use being that they would allow for the vessel to be strung up. The 'aryballos' is a phial of globular shape, also having diminutive handles inserted immediately below the rim and ending at the shoulder of the vessel, often with a tiny ornate finial snaking upward. The 'amphora' belongs to the third group, has a balus-troid body, a longer, more pronounced neck with handles of the same length and a pointed base, ending in a button or tiny disc-shaped foot which serves no practical purpose. To the last group belongs the 'oino-choe', the only vessel that does have a foot to stand on. It is shaped like a small jug, with a lipped mouth usually formed by pinching in the hot metal, and a handle.

The first colours used on these small glass vessels were the blues as a base, with perhaps just one other colour laid on. With the passing centuries glassmakers became more enterprising and a variety of colours were applied to cored vessels. A deep blue and turquoise were almost always predominant. Copper was used as a colouring agent to obtain greens and blues, and copper mines were easily accessible.

The domination of Egypt by Alexander, paradoxically, benefited the Egyptian glass industry. The city of Alexandria became the focal point of cultural and industrial life and a glassmaking centre was established which profited greatly by the influx of craftsmen from other glass factories in Egypt and Syria. During the Ptolemaic period (323–30 B.C.), Alexandrian glass became a luxury article exported to countries all over the world, some as remote as Scandinavia. The millefiori and mosaic bowls dating from the second and first centuries B.C. were still made for a hundred years or so after the beginning of the Christian era. They are direct descendants of the millefiori glass technique developed by the Egyptians of the XVIIIth Dynasty (1500–1400 B.C.) but now the technique benefited by advanced knowledge and larger availability of colouring agents, and a gaily coloured effect was created. Larger objects such as dishes and vases were made of glass imitating the effect of natural stone and agates. This was achieved by fusing layers of different coloured glass, resulting in the development of a cased glass that could be cut cameo-fashion. Engraving and cutting became an added feature of first century B.C. Alexandrian glassware, and relief and intaglio cutting was accomplished relatively well, due to the influence of experienced Greek and Roman gem cutters. The earlier mentioned Portland Vase in the British Museum is the finest surviving example of first century cameo-cut glass. This two-handled urn of dark-blue glass is overlaid by an opaque white casing which has been cut away and the figures, representing characters from Greek mythology, are modelled in exquisite relief against their dark background. In 1845 the vase and its case were "shattered to atoms" by William Lloyd, a young Irishman, who could give no explanation for his outrageous action but so impressed the judge with his frankness and "respectable appearance" that he was let off with fine of £3 and never heard of again. The vase was painstakingly reassembled and finally, in 1945, it was bought from its owner, the Duke of Portland, by the Trustees of the British Museum.

The few existing examples of similar style and technique as the Portland Vase have all been found in Italy.

Syria and Rome

Early Syrian glass sites have not revealed large quantities of finds. Some cored vessels of the later period, from 600 B.C., show development on parallel lines with Egypt, and techniques also include moulding and carving from a solid glass block. 'The Sargon' vase at the British Museum is one of the few datable pieces in a good state of survival. It is pear-shaped and about 4 in. high. Originally of transparent greenish glass it is now opaque with a slight green and silver iridescence beneath the flaking brownish enamel-like weathering. On one side it is decorated with an engraved lion and the name of Sargon II, king of Assyria (722–705 B.C.) in cuneiform characters; two small 'ears' project from the shoulders. It is a thick glass and has been carved from a block and hollowed out.

It is generally accepted that glassblowing was developed by Syrian glassmakers about the first century A.D. and that they brought their new technique to Alexandria. A quantity of mould-blown vessels have been found in Syria and conveniently some of the ancient glassblowers were sufficiently proud of their work to add their signature to some suitable motto inscribed in the mould. The most famous of this group of early glass-blowers was one Ennion. Other prominent names are those of Jason, Meges and Neikaios; a cup by the last mentioned bears the appealing moulded inscription, in Greek: "Neikaios made me—Let the buyer remember. Wherefore thou art come, rejoice." Ennion's work is decidedly Hellenistic in feeling and the widely distributed finds, ranging from Italy and the Greek Islands to North Africa and the Russian port of Kerch, suggest that Ennion and his group either moved their workshops to Northern Italy or sent out their own workmen to establish subsidiary glasshouses outside Syria. This theory is well supported by the migratory character of Syrian artisans who were sufficiently ambitious to seize any offered opportunity to improve their status. Syrian glasshouses were established in many areas of the European Roman Empire, but the quality of Syrian glass never quite approached that of Alexandrian manufacture. For moulding small objects glass pastes were used, but the soda glass of Syrian glassmaking centres, as at Sidon for instance, was eminently suitable for blowing. A certain originality was developed by the Syrian glassblowers and is shown in the so-called 'relief glasses' made during the second and third centuries A.D. These are phials and small jugs in the form of fruit or animals. An especially attractive section is represented by the 'head-bottles', mould blown so that the main body of the flask forms the shape of a human head. The glass metal is usually coloured and transparent; colourless glass for vessels did not come into general use until sometime during the second century A.D. A large number of Alexandrian glassworkers settled in Antioch and brought the technique of the 'early Christian' gold glasses to Syria. Much of this Zwischengold glass was found in Roman catacombs and because some of the decorative subjects imply a religious theme, ancient gold glass is often referred to as early Christian or Jewish. It may have been manufactured for ritual use but decorative motifs also include plant and flower designs in attractive, graceful patterns. Glass was valued as highly as gold and we are told of a procession held in honour of the Emperor Darius, which included a presentation display of glass tables decorated with gold leaf. The Zwischengold technique lingered on until the fifth century.

While in Egypt luxury glass manufacture was on the decline, Syrian glass decoration became more elaborate from the third to the seventh century. Coloured transparent glass blobs and threads were applied to the object's surface, sometimes zigzag patterns would cover the entire vessel. The plasticity of the Syrian soda metal favoured this type of ornamental treatment and the seventeenth-century Venetians were seduced by this very same quality of their own soda-cristallo glass to even more exaggerated fantasies. Syrian glassmakers did not favour the art of cutting in the same way as did their Alexandrian neighbours. They preferred to produce coloured elaborate glassware, whereas the accent in Alexandria was on more classical lines and there was a considerable output of colourless glass.

The earliest Roman efforts at blowing glass resulted in bottles or flasks of simple shape, with free-blown bulbous body, longish cylindrical neck with projecting rim, mostly without handles. 'Unguentaria' such as the so-called 'tear-bottles', the small club-formed phials, supposedly receptacles for the tears of mourners, are common funerary finds (plate facing p. 17).

Glass was made in Europe during the period of Roman colonization in a confusing variety of design and style. The technique was introduced by artisans following in the wake of the Roman legions, passing on the knowledge acquired in some distant part of the Roman Empire. According to the location of glasshouses, if known, glass made in Europe during this period may be termed Seine–Rhine or Gallic, or Rhenish. The distinctive 'snake thread' decoration, consisting of milled or notched glass threads of various colours applied in spiral or looped patterns, has been found in Syria and the Cologne region. The group found in Germany is refreshingly referred to by the late W. A. Thorpe (*English Glass*, London, 1935) as the product of 'Snake Thread (Rhine) Ltd.'. Work by followers or pupils of Ennion's glass-blowing school is particularly attractive in the pictorial

57

mould-blown glass vessels of clear greenish or amber metal, the so-called chariot or gladiator cups. These glass cups are decorated with subjects relating to the Roman arena—chariots, circuses and wild animals encircle the surface, usually in two or three horizontally divided strips. They were most probably produced in Gallic glasshouses. Similar scenes have been found painted on glass vessels and are attributed to North Italian manufacture. Both these groups date from the first and second centuries. Christian subjects became popular later, during the fourth century.

With the adoption of glass blowing, the practicality of the Roman mind comes to the fore and the typical Roman flask of functional design makes its appearance in all areas of the Seine–Rhine appropriations. Handles were a logical consequence of the necessity of transport and the reeded handle of angular design, which may terminate in a small scroll or loop during the late Roman period, is one of the most elegant features of this vessel. By the second century a fairly uniform shape developed with the square flask with reeded handle(s), the most suitable vessel for packing and transportation. The cylindrical and barrel-shaped flasks also retained their popularity and by the late second and early third centuries more imaginative decorative techniques appeared. Wrythen and mould-blown decorations of the nipped diamond waies (NDW) type and chain handles are characteristic for Seine–Rhine glass development at this period. It is not unusual to find the maker's mark in the form of initials or full names on flasks and bottles. Frontinus, probably working in Northern France during the early third century, seems to have been manufacturing glass bottles on a considerable scale and blowing some flasks in two-part moulds in attractive ribbed pattern, imitating barrel hoops. The metal of bottle glass deteriorated and later Roman vessels are blown rather thin and embellished with trails of predominantly blue colour applied to handles and neck. The long-necked Syrian dropper with several connecting funnels, a bottle, which pours very slowly due to its exceptionally narrow orifice, makes its appearance about the fourth century. It is the forefather of the Eastern long-necked sprinkler bottle and the German spiral-necked Angster or Kuttrolf, both developed during the sixteenth century. Glass of the early Roman period was produced in a variety of colours, but by the second century a greenish-coloured metal became apparent. The amply wooded areas favoured potash glass production and the result was a greenish or yellow-greenish metal of occasionally bubbly transparency. This is the Seine–Rhine Waldglas or Forest glass—the French *Verre de Fougère*. Waldglas retained its popularity far into the fifteenth century, and was produced even after the development of the Venetian cristallo glass. In common with cristallo it was replaced by the newly developed lead crystal.

A certain quantity of luxury glass was still imported from Alexandria and has been found on early military sites or during excavations of villas. Shallow dishes, moulded and ground, were made in strong, translucent colours of blue and green but opaque red, blue and white glass has also been found in smaller quantities; mosaic glass was rarely exported from Alexandria.

Cups and bowls decorated by a highly accomplished technique of facet-cutting have been found in widely separated areas of the Roman Empire. They date from the late first or second century A.D. and have been cut from moulded blanks with predominantly lozenge-shaped pattern design. The greenish, colourless metal and the curvilinear engraved band below the rim are typical features of this group of glasses.

With the 'Vasa Diatreta', or cage-cup, the glass cutter had reached the summit of his art. Cage-cups are assumed products of the late Roman Empire and although Western in concept, the patience required for carrying out such highly complicated technique points to some oriental influence. Cage-cups are made of cased glass and mostly ovoid in shape. The body is of white or greenish transparent metal with the lower part surrounded by a delicately cut network, usually of coloured glass. The upper half of the vessel is generally encircled by an inscription which is undercut in the same manner as the carved network and attached to the wall of the cup by struts, remaining for this purpose. The carved inscription might represent the owner's name or some pleasing motto and introduces a third colour. The delicate and ornamental effect achieved in these cups has no equal in glass history. The largest number of cage-cups have been found in the Rhine area and their date of manufacture is somewhere between the first and third centuries A.D. In view of the oriental aspect of this work and the later Eastern appropriations the more likely date would tend to be the third century. The fourth-century 'Lycurgus' cup, acquired for the British Museum in 1958, presents one of the finest and most realistic examples of cage-cup techniques in existence. It is attributed to Italian workmanship and represents Lycurgus in the act of being strangled by the maenad Ambrosia as she is changing into a vine. The glass is green with a patch of yellow and in transmitted light changes to ruby and amethyst, an as yet unexplained fact, though possibly connected with the presence of minute gold particles in the metal. The carving, surrounding the cup in one continuous frieze, bears a striking resemblance to the techniques applied to oriental jade and this impression is further enhanced by the colour effect of the glass (plate facing p. 16).

Coloured blobs were applied not only by Syrian but also by Roman glassworkers and one of their particular methods of decoration consisted of contrast coloured blobs applied all over the soft paraison and marvered in before being expanded blown. This first-century technique was applied in a slightly varied form to fourth-century Roman beakers. The method was to apply a line of blobs just below the rim of the vessel, and these were marvered smooth without further blowing.

Mediaeval Europe

The technique of applied blobs or 'prunts' outlived the period of Roman domination and found expression, somewhat exaggeratedly, in the claw beaker (*Rüssel-Becher*) perfected to a considerable extent during the Frankish–Merovingian period. Applied blobs and prunts are mostly found on drinking vessels and their original function was to assist a firm grip on the handle-less beaker. Cone-shaped beakers with horizontal or vertical applied trails were a Seine–Rhine product of the fifth century. The cone-shaped base ensured that the glass was empty before it could be set down, resting on the rim. The shape of claw beakers gradually evolved a more blown-out silhouette and by the seventh and eighth centuries the elaborate claw-foot beaker had been established. The metal was either greenish yellow or deep green, and the design still incorporated spiral trails. A flat base was still not large enough to induce stability and claws were applied in alternate tiers. The complicated technique involved in the making of such claw-foot beakers is perhaps not fully realized. The claw is applied in the form of a hot glass blob to the cooled surface of the vessel. The surface softens at the point of impact and the gaffer quickly blows into his paraison. His breath makes a hole at the softened site and inflates the blob. When a satisfactory bulge has been achieved the servitor uses a sharp tool to hook the expanded blob outwards and downwards, and then presses the tip on to the surface of the beaker one or two inches below. Quite often the claws themselves are further embellished by applied notched trails of coloured glass (plate facing p. 17).

By the eighth century Western European glassmaking had entered a phase variously described as 'The Empty Ages' or 'The Mediaeval Slump'. This sudden and lengthy decline of the glass industry was due to a variety of causes, economic, political and secular. The industrial prowess of the foreign elements introduced by Roman colonization gave rise to misgivings on behalf of the native artisans and merchants. Syrian and Jewish business acumen and craftsmanship made itself felt not only in the glass industry and a wave of antisemitism was the result. This was not a conflict between Jews and the Church, but a fear of impending serious depression in the national economy. The consequent persecutions and deprivation of glassmakers of semitic background put an eventual end to a flourishing glass industry and the fact that the Church, from whom support was expected, forbade the use of glass vessels for ritual purposes terminated all hopes for the establishment of a new, native glass industry.

Pre-Islam and Islamic Glass

Constantine I (A.D. 274–337) established Byzantium as the new capital of the Eastern half of the Roman Empire. The city's wealth attracted all kinds of artisans from the West who found both affluence and protection there. Theodosius II (A.D. 408–450) exempted glassmakers from all taxes, a privilege that had already been extended by Constantine to the glaziers settled at Cologne. One aspect of a flourishing Byzantine glass art has been preserved in the magnificent mosaics at Ravenna, where the portraits of Justinian (527–65) and his empress Theodora are represented in stylized splendour on the walls of the Church of San Vitale. Justinian divided his glassworkers into vitrarii and diatretarii and in this way distinguished the artist from the craftsman. Wheel-cutting was ably carried out by Byzantine diatretarii and tesselated patterns of round or oval facets was a decorative method practised throughout Persia and Mesopotamia in pre- and post-Islamic time.

An important section of glassmaking was directed towards the manufacture of coloured window glass and the influence of mosaic art is again unmistakable. A method still in use was to perforate marble slabs or plasterwork to form certain patterns and fill the voids with coloured glass pieces of smallish size. Flowers, trees and simple vessels (vases) are commonly represented by the window pattern. The iconoclastic movement initiated by Leo III in A.D. 726 resulted in much of this splendid work being destroyed.

Despite a flourishing industry almost no decorative glass of the early Byzantine period has survived. Several cups and basins of greenish wheel-cut glass are preserved at St. Mark's in Venice and incorporate some enamelling. The Sacro Catino Dish at Genoa, a hexagonally shaped footed cup with handles, was originally thought to be an emerald but turned out to be a green glass with many minute air bubbles. During the sacking of Constantinople by Venetians and French in 1204 many such treasures were plundered and much so-called Byzantine glass is of relatively late date. A table of solid emerald with three golden feet was part of the booty taken by the Arab commander Musa, together with other treasures captured from Toledo. An inscription supposedly in Greek seems to indicate that this marvel was probably nothing else but a table made of Byzantine glass. This incident must have taken place during A.D. 710–20, when Spain fell as one of their last conquests to the Moslem invaders. In 634 the Byzantine armies were defeated and the creation of a huge Islamic Empire had begun. By A.D. 750 the Moslem-dominated areas stretched from Turkestan through Armenia, Persia, Syria, Arabia, Egypt and along the North African coast to Spain. It embraced all the important glassmaking centres of the Eastern sphere.

The nomadic tribes which swelled the nucleus of Moslem invaders were not endowed with any particular native art or craft. The art of Islam was purely ornamental and, in its earliest phase, abstract; national characteristics did not develop until about the tenth century, with a prolific industry during the thirteenth and fourteenth centuries and a decline by the sixteenth. Craftsmen were annexed from the most important cultural centres within the vast empire and the main glass industries flourished again in Syria and Egypt.

A series of transparent, coloured glass weights or tokens in the British Museum are stamped with the names of Egyptian Caliphs during A.D. 760 and 1225. During the ninth century a glass industry was centred near the town of Samarra in Iraq and the excavated glass fragments of varying techniques show the influence of foreign craftsmen. Relief cutting found on fragments was introduced by Egyptian artisans and resembles Egyptian rock crystal cutting. Both engraved and cut stylized designs of Papyrus and Lotus plants are of the early Islamic period and a variety of other techniques, such as for instance cased glass and an inlaid combed thread decoration, have been identified from finds made in Syria and Egypt. In his travel tales Benjamin of Tudela describes a reappearing glass industry in Syria during the twelfth century and he tells of the glassmakers at Antioch and of four hundred Jews at New Tyre, who continued the traditions of the Tyrian glass manufacture. With more colourful imagination he described the great Mosque at Damascus, supposedly incorporating one wall of glass with as many openings as there are days in the year, in order that the sun's rays might fall in gradual succession through each opening in turn.

During the eleventh century Egypt developed an interesting type of glass decoration known as lustre-painting. Vessels of this group are relatively rare and are distinguished by a lustrous pigment. The decoration is usually carried out in monochrome but there are rare examples of colour variations on the same piece. The precise techniques of this lustrous film on glass objects has not yet been identified but lustre-painting of pottery was well understood in the East and doubtless there must be some connection with this method.

An individual style of linear-type relief cutting is represented in the fascinating group of glass beakers known as 'Hedwig' glasses. Hedwig, a patron saint of Silesia and Poland, died in 1243, and one of these vessels, supposedly belonging to the saint, is now preserved in the museum at Wroclaw, formerly Breslau. The survival of these glasses, some dozen or so, is due to their having been used as reliquaries and it is possible we are indebted to the crusaders for their appearance in Europe. Hedwig beakers are made of thick, somewhat bubbly glass which is transparent with a slight smoky green or topaz tinge. Stylized animal forms, such as lions, eagles or griffins, are typical for Hedwig glass and the deep wheel-cutting is relieved by hatched engraved lines representing the details of the design. They are dated about the eleventh or twelfth century, even though the glass preserved at the Rijks Museum, Amsterdam, bears the inscription: "When this glass was a thousand years old, it was presented to the Count Palatine Ludwig Philip. 1634." Much speculation centres about these glasses, which are so identical in treatment and metal that they must have been made in the same workshop. The technique is attributed to Egyptian craftsmen but the decorative design does strike distinctly Byzantine. One of the glasses incorporates a crescent moon, an emblem adopted by Byzantium and symbolizing the flash of lightning which revealed the advancing Macedonian army and gave the beleaguered city a chance of deliverance from the siege. A more recent speculation comes from Russia where, on the basis of excavations, the style of these cups is related to the art of twelfth-century Kiev. They belong to the most impressive groups of early glasses and are often of equally generous proportions; the specimen at the British Museum measures about 5½ in. high and has a diameter at the top of just over 5 in. (pl. facing p. 32).

With the rise of Islam to a world power we speak of the emergence of a characteristic Islamic style in the decorative arts. A piece of glass catalogued as 'in the Islamic style' is usually understood to be enamelled and gilded in the ornamentally stylized manner associated with the Syrian glass centres of Raqqa and Aleppo, prolific during A.D. 1170–1270 and 1250–65. The techniques carried out in these workshops consisted of three individual stages and after each stage the glass to be decorated was reintro-

enetian standing cup of the early
mid-15th century. Sapphire blue
ass enamelled in various colours
ightened by gilding, representing
triumphal procession of Venus.
he stem and foot show decorative
rinkling with gold dust. Ht. 16·5 cm.

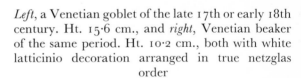

Left, a Venetian goblet of the late 17th or early 18th
century. Ht. 15·6 cm., and *right*, Venetian beaker
of the same period. Ht. 10·2 cm., both with white
latticinio decoration arranged in true netzglas
order

Mid-16th-century French goblet. Colourless horny glass, enamelled and gilt. Probably a marriage goblet, it shows a man and a woman and the inscriptions: "Ie svis a vovs" (*Je suis à vous*) and "Mō cvevr aves" (*Mon coeur à vous*), "Iehan Bovcav. et. Antoynette Bovc". A goat drinking water represents the name "Bouc eau". Ht. 16·2 cm.

A late-17th-century French beaker, attributed to Bernard Perrot of Orléans. Mould-blown, clear, greyish glass. Ornamentation represents a couple holding hands, a sun face, a rampant horse and three fleurs-de-lys. Ht. 7·2 cm.

duced into the muffle kiln for firing. In the first stage the ornamental pattern was applied by the artist in gold leaf. After firing the outline of the design was traced in red and when this was fired enamelled colours were finally applied and again annealed. Most Islamic enamel is of translucent colour except for white, which is opaque. The earliest Islamic enamelled glass was made at Raqqa, but the town was destroyed by the Mongols in A.D. 1259 and glass manufacture consequently declined. In the meantime Aleppo had developed into an important glass industry centre and the best enamelled work was done there during the mid-thirteenth century. Aleppo enamelled glass shows more refinement and ingenuity than the Raqqa product, which is distinguished by slightly more crude application of the enamel, often in thick blobs, and a more primitive style of design. In time Islamic laws became more lenient toward figurative representation and this emerges quite distinctly with the decorative design on Aleppo enamelled ware. Hunters and musicians, birds, beasts, flowers and trees are often found framed in cartouches of medallion shape or sur-rounded by arabesque forms. Enamelled decoration of trefoil design or three leaves with separate stems are associated with Aleppo manufacture and are seen on bottles, goblets and pilgrim flasks of the mid-thirteenth century. The shape most notably associated with thirteenth-century Aleppo glass is the flared enamelled beaker, of which the 'Luck of Eden-hall' is one of the best-known examples. The more delicately enamelled glasses and goblets with pictorial ornamentation in the style of Persian miniatures are attributed to Damascene manufacture. A flourishing in-dustry existed in Damascus since about 1250, which was enriched perhaps by a Chinese influence at the end of the thirteenth century, the time of Mongol infiltration. Glass à la façon de Damas became greatly valued in mediaeval Europe and Court circles. The Saracen Mosque lamps are exceptionally fine examples of Damascene work and almost all specimens show a similar design in the wide body, outsplayed neck and flared wide mouth. Very early fourteenth-century lamps display three suspension rings on the body, the later type, from the middle of the fourteenth century, having six applied. Mosque lamps are usually blown from transparent greenish or yellowish tinged colourless glass but occasionally a blue or green metal is used. The rich enamelling is divided into bands of inscriptions in cursative Arabic 'naskh' script, interrupted by cartouches and medallions of floral or figurative theme. The ornamental inscription usually refers to verses of the Koran, and includes the name of the Sultan by whom the lamp was ordered and the Mosque where it is to be displayed. Occasionally the artist added his name and sometimes the inscription is composed of meaningless symbols applied purely as a form of decoration. (Plate facing p. 32.)

With the incursion of the Mongols and the sack of Damascus by Tamerlane in 1402, the industry fell into a decline. At this time another element was fully prepared to step into the void, the great maritime city of Venice. Venetian influence on later Persian glass of the sixteenth, seventeenth and eighteenth centuries has produced some pleasing shapes and the industry was revived with the help of Italian gaffers. The best glass was made in the factory established at Shiraz, with a deep blue as the most popular colour (plate facing p. 40).

Development and Significance of Stained Glass

The stained window presents a perfect bridge from Eastern to Western glass art. It came to Europe via Byzantium and the Eastern Church and appeared as early as the ninth century in St. Peter's and Santa Maria, Travetere Roma. According to a letter written by the Abbot Gozbert, a studio of glass-painters was in existence in 999 in his monastery on the Tegernsee, not far from Munich. The same monastery records the glass-painting activities of a monk, Wernherus, during the eleventh century. A little later we have the invaluable description of the art by Theophilus in his *Diversarum Artium Schedulae*, about A.D. 1100. The glass painter would draw the picture to be represented in actual size on a large trestle table and mark the colours and lead strips accordingly. He would then cut out the desired shape of the glass pieces by marking the outline with a hot iron and dropping water on the heated areas. The glass would crack at the marked point and could be broken into the required shape. The diamond was not used for cutting window-glass until about A.D. 1500 and, if necessary, the glass piece was cut to shape with the 'grozing iron', a notched instrument similar to a spanner. The overpainting on the coloured (pot-metal) glass pieces was carried out in Schwarzlot, a low viscosity mixture prepared from copper oxide (later from scale) and powdered glass. Schwarzlot was also used for shading or blackening entire surfaces and a sgraffito-like ornamental effect was achieved by abrasion or scraping off. The glass panes treated by this method were fired and the design safely fused to the glass. After annealing, the individual panes were inserted into strips of lead, the calmes (Latin *calamus*=reed). These strips were soldered at the joints and the glass panes cemented in between the grooves. A large window was difficult to set in its frame because of its fragility. It was there-fore supported by an iron grille, necessary also for static reasons, and the grille itself was used, as were also the lead strips, to emphasize the orna-mental design of the window.

The earliest coloured glass windows were ornamental rather than figurative and plant ornaments, medallions and pastiches formed a bril-liant pattern in the manner of the oriental carpet. The twelfth-century window, with its innumerable small pieces of coloured glass, is represented in Abbot Suger's church at Saint Denis. This technique, which preserves its Eastern-influenced mosaic character, persisted throughout Western France well into the thirteenth century (Chartres, Poitiers). The thirteenth century brings a profusion of brilliant coloured glass windows on the Continent and in England. The French influence is often so marked that it is impossible to state whether a window was decorated by an artist trained in France and working in his native land or whether the entire work was a foreign import.

An outstanding technique employed during the thirteenth century was that of the 'grisaille' glass, supposed to have been initiated by the Cister-cian Order, whose austere beliefs would not allow coloured or figurative window glass. Grisaille windows were made of white glass with Schwarzlot painted decorative motifs. The ornamental pattern was formed solely by the varied shapes of the leaded glass pieces. Ingenious introduction of pieces of potmetal in red, blue, green and yellow produced an extraordi-narily attractive and artistic effect which is admirably exemplified in the beautiful Five Sisters' Window in York Minster, completed between 1250–

60. During the fourteenth century naturalistic patterns of trees and leaves appeared, and leads served to emphasize the outline of the painted ornament. The industry grew and rapidly became organized with each man specializing in a set task. The master glazier would draw the design which was painted by the artist. The grozier cut the glass and the joynour or closour would fit the panes into the lead 'calmes'. Centres of glaziers and glasspainters are recorded in larger cities, notably Oxford, York, London, Exeter, Norwich and King's Lynn, and often a foundation was laid to a future industry on domestic lines. At that time the master designer would draw his design on parchment or paper cartoons, often using them again and again with slight colour changes or by ingeniously reversing the figures and altering the features by addition of a beard, or garment. Heraldic design, too, makes its appearance and inscriptions are added. The circular medallion becomes almond-shaped, the carpet-like background disappears and a new influence from England sweeps across Europe by way of Belgium and Northern France to the Rhineland and Switzerland. The late gothic design is characterized by pictorial unity emphasized by framing of architectural dimension.

The fifteenth century brought several new advances in the techniques of coloured glass painting. The most important of these was the 'yellow stain', produced by covering the glass surface with a film of silver nitrate and subsequent annealing. The variation of colour tone which could be achieved by this method ranged from light-brownish to a brilliant orange found in early sixteenth-century windows. A bright emerald green resulted from the application of the silver nitrate method on panes of potmetal blue. At this time a more sculptural effect was obtained by the innovation of grinding away the red overlay glaze wherever desired. Towards the year 1500 a new, third glass paint was developed, the 'Eisenrot' (German *Eisen* = iron, *rot* = red), and shading and modelling was now applied quite successfully. In 1505 Barnard Flower 'de Alemania' was appointed King's Glazier and after doing work at Westminster he was naturalized in 1514. After his death in 1517 other glaziers were charged to continue his work, notably at the King's College Chapel in Cambridge. Several of the artists were of Flemish or German origin. By the early seventeenth century the actual art of the stained-glass window begins its decline. The civil wars in England and in the Lorraine, the region supplying much of the necessary coloured glass, impoverished the industry. Germany had great difficulty in producing a potmetal of the essential deep colour at that time, and to produce the necessary red overlay glaze. A further factor responsible for the decline of stained glass was the development of large-size panes in a sparkling transparent glass. The industries of France, Spain and Italy met with a similar fate. England and Switzerland held out longer against the new fashion for transparent white window-glass, but even so glass-painting lost its essential characteristics due to the desire of the artist to produce a painting on glass rather than a stained-glass window.

The metamorphosis of stained glass to pictures painted on glass was most successfully represented in its transitional period by the Swiss work of the sixteenth and seventeenth centuries. Glass-painting aimed in an entirely different direction and developed into an art created specifically to satisfy the demands of the private citizen. This trend is represented by a type of domestic 'Kabinett-Malerei' or 'Klein-Malerei', applied in translucent enamel-like colours, and often based on designs by artists such as Holbein, Burkmair and Urs Graf. This particular glass art was immensely popular from the fifteenth to the seventeenth century and emphasized the Swiss custom of donating commemorative windows and presenting heraldic arms. The glass pieces were produced in larger sizes so that one complete theme or illustration could be represented on one single pane. In consequence the picture lost its mosaic character and there was a gradual diminishing of the application of lead surrounds. The subjects represented were not confined solely to colourful heraldry, but landscapes and figures of naturalistic concept appeared on the transparent white glass pane. Biblical and mythological subjects were freely expressed in this 'small-art', and with the transition to Baroque and Rococo a type of genre painting developed. This influenced the entire concept of painting on glass and we see the emergence of the glass picture destined not to embellish the window but the wall. This change also conditioned the character of the paints themselves. The glowing transparent enamels disappeared to give way to a lustreless opaque paint. The theatrical taste of the Rococo period is recalled by the square glass-pictures of the eighteenth century, which consisted of two glass panes placed one behind the other. The first represented the foreground to a stage setting, or the actual stage scene, the second formed a background to the picture, the whole conveying the impression of a theatrical tableau.

Glass and mirror pictures were popular during the seventeenth and eighteenth centuries. With the Rococo taste for 'Chinoiserie' it became the fashion to decorate mirrors in the Chinese style. In many cases the mirror itself was of Western manufacture, exported and embellished by a Chinese artist, and reintroduced into the Western home. The usual method was to remove the silvered backing from the desired areas and to paint the picture on the underside. For the artist this meant that he had to apply his colour-effects in the reverse order, a feat in which the Chinese were particularly skilful. Similar effects were achieved by the method of transfer pictures, whereby an uncoloured engraving was fixed on to the underside of the glass by means of a transparent, adhesive varnish. When the varnish had dried completely the paper was damped and carefully rubbed away so that all that remained on the glass was a faint impression of the print. The picture was then realistically coloured. A variety of related techniques derived in the main from the ancient *Zwischengold* or *fondi d'oro* methods were applied to glass. An elaboration of this process is the *verre églomisé*, developed during the Baroque movement which emanated from Italy. The method consisted of the application of gold leaf to the reverse side of the glass and engraving on it a design by means of a needle. The entire gold leaf was then covered with a black or other contrasting colour which accentuated the engraved picture. In common with the ancient method, the decoration was protected from the back by a thin layer of glass or any other suitable medium such as a coating of durable lacquer varnish. Gold leaf, combined with glowing reds and greens, made the most effective colour-schemes, which heightened the flowing ebullience of Baroque design.

The ultimate result of the metamorphosis from stained glass to glass pictures are the black and sepia (Schwarzlot) enamels of Johann Schader (1621–70), working in Nürnberg, Preissler's work of the early eighteenth century and the translucent enamels produced during the early nineteenth century by the Mohns of Dresden and Kothgasser of Vienna. Both Mohns, father and son, began as window glass painters and invented their own paints. The son, Gottlob Samuel Mohn, supplied the windows to the Chapel of the Emperor's Castle in Laxenburg, lower Austria. He also painted the windows of the Church Maria Stiegen in Vienna.

With the fall of Damascus, the great tradition of Islamic enamelled glass expired and during the following two centuries the monopoly of ornamental glass was ably and tantalizingly held by Venice.

Venetian Glass

Venice has the distinction that her glasshouses formed the nucleus of a revived glass art which spread over Renaissance Europe and laid the foundation for a new glassmaking industry. Her indispensable contribution to the development of decorative glass consisted of several ingenious processes most of which were a revival, or perfection, of a lost art.

The first of these was the rediscovered art of enamelling which had been a pronounced Islamic decorative method until the onset of a general regression in the industry after the fall of Damascus. The second Venetian development, the rediscovery of decolourizing agents such as manganese dioxide, resulted in a transparent colourless glassmetal of particular pliability and led to the creation of light and airy shapes associated with glass *à la façon de Venise*. The third Venetian contribution of far-reaching effect was the perfection of the latticinio technique, which inspired in its ultimate form the enamel twist stem.

Glass had been manufactured in Venice for several centuries before her industry became a permanent settlement on the Isle of Murano in 1291. The city of Venice was founded about A.D. 420 by families from Acquileia and Padua who had fled from Attila's huns and found refuge among the islands of the lagoons. It has been claimed that glassmaking had been practised since the foundation of the city but there exists no substantiating evidence. The church of St. Mark's at Venice provides a link between the cultures of East and West and was originally planned as a Byzantine church. In 829, upon the demolition of St. Mark's at Alexandria by

Mohammedans, the relics were acquired by the Doge of Venice, who planned the building of a cathedral to enshrine them. However, St. Mark's was not completed until Gothic times, and work on the famous mosaics was continued over a period of 250 years. Venetian craftsmen are recorded as being employed on the mosaics in 1159, and in the next century the glassworkers, or 'Phiolari', drew up certain trading regulations pertaining to their craft. While in other parts of Italy, such as Rome and Siena, the industry concentrated on mosaic work, ornamental glass was successfully manufactured in Venice. Natural assets of location, business acumen and a powerful navy assured the unrivalled position of the new republic on the Adriatic. In its flourishing glass industry Venice saw a further source for amassing foreign gold. The transfer of the industry to Murano was carried out not only in the interest of safety but as a measure for ensuring that none of the processes of Venetian glassmaking would leak out to any foreign industry. Admirers of Venetian glass were forced to buy from the source and glass export became a flourishing trade. In 1399 Richard II gave permission to the masters of two Venetian merchant ships anchored in the Port of London to sell their glass on board, duty-free. In 1542 an inventory of Henry VIII's property at Westminster listed 450 diverse objects of glass, such as "great glasses like bolles standing upon fete, great bell candlestickes, glasses with long smale neckes and great bellies and a layer of blewe glasses partly gilt, the layer having the Kinge's Armes gilt upon it."

The stringent laws governing the lives of Murano glass workers were no empty threats. The arm of justice was long and any workman who dared carry his art abroad was, after due warning, liable to persecution and death. In Normandy a Murano glassmaker, Paoli, was found by his daughter with a dagger in his heart and a note 'traitor' attached. There are records of similar incidents as late as the eighteenth century. Happily such gruesome examples could not entirely deter the Murano glassworker, and the promise of greater reward and more favourable conditions led many a gaffer to foreign soil. In addition the rival glass industry at Altare, near Genoa, was not subjected to such severe regulations; on the contrary, workers were encouraged to make yearly journeys outside their own pro-

Colourless Nürnberg glass goblet. Wheel-engraved decoration by Herman Schwinger consists of bacchanalian scenes and verses on the bowl and laurel leaf and berry circuit on the foot; signed, *c.* 1665. Ht. 27·8 cm.

Nürnberg footed beaker, decorated in Schwarzlot by Johann Schaper and signed with his monogram. The portrait represents the Elector of Cologne, Maximilian Henry, Duke of Bavaria; *c.* 1660–70. Ht. 8·2 cm.

Late-16th-century Bohemian Humpen. The clear glass has a greyish tint and the enamelled decoration represents a hunting scene. Ht. 26·2 cm.

Beaker made in the Southern Netherlands, second half of the 16th century. Ice-glass ornamented with three gilt lion masks and intermediate prunts with blue glass pearls. Ht. 20·9 cm.

A Russian or Bohemian beaker of the late 18th century in thick, clear, greenish glass containing numerous bubbles and impurities with crude engraving showing remnants of gilding. The design represents the double-headed eagle with sceptre and orb, the whole encircled by sun-rays and surmounted by a crown. Ht. 8·7 cm.

English glasses : *above, left to right,* inverted baluster glass, 1700–20. Ht. 15·3 cm. ; a jelly glass, 1740–
Ht. 10 cm. ; Silesian stem wineglass, *c.* 1720. Ht. 15·7 cm. ; patch stand, *c.* 1720. Ht. 5·5 cm. ; sweetm⟨eat⟩
conventionally 1690. Ht. 10 cm. ; *below,* Jacobite 'Fiat' glass, drawn-airtwist trumpet, wheel-engrav⟨ed⟩
c. 1750. Ht. 15·5 cm. ; mixed air and enamel twist wineglass with double ogee bowl, 1760–70. ⟨Ht.⟩
16·5 cm. ; enamel twist wineglass, *c.* 1760. Ht. 15·2 cm. ; wineglass, airtwist stem, *c.* 1750. Ht. 15·7 c⟨m.⟩
wineglass, faceted stem, *c.* 1770. Ht. 14·2 cm. ; Light Newcastle baluster friendship glass. Dutch wh⟨eel⟩
engraving, two-sectional stem, centre knop enclosing tears, 1745–50. Ht. 19 cm.

vinces. There was little difference between glass of Altarist manufacture and the product of Murano and definite attribution to one or the other is not possible.

Glassworkers were divided into four distinctive groups. The 'phiolari' made vessels and window glass, the 'specchiai' were mirror-makers and the 'cristallai' concentrated on making optical glass. The most ancient craft of all was practised by the fourth group, the bead-makers, who again were subdivided according to their particular speciality. The 'paternostreri' appropriately made rosaries, the 'margitai' small beads, probably by marvering, and the 'fuppialume' manufactured large beads by blowing. Glassworkers were highly esteemed by Venetian society and formed their own guilds and fraternities. They were considered gentlemen, though by no means noblemen. Nevertheless, no nobleman or woman was disgraced by associating with a glassmaker and his family, an idea which is carried a little further by the French *gentilhomme verrier*.

Venetian glass of the early Renaissance shows the distinct influence of Gothic style. Goblets, tazza and ewers are of austere form and fairly thick metal. The practical mind of the Italian gaffer produced the 'folded' foot, a method of strengthening the foot of glass vessels by folding the soft glass under to obtain a rim of double thickness. The pedestal stem with spreading folded foot and the applied frilled or gadrooned trail surrounding the base of the bowl are characteristic of the glass produced from the mid-fifteenth to the early sixteenth century (plate facing p. 33). Murano glass of richly coloured metal was made for a short period only, before it was superseded by the new colourless cristallo. Sapphire blue (pl. facing p. 64) and emerald green were favoured colours, but a purple was also made. Cristallo was not in common use until the beginning of the sixteenth century but a certain group of luxury glasses such as presentation covered goblets and tazza with rich enamelling and gilding were made of colourless transparent glass during the second half of the fifteenth century. One of the earliest coloured pieces is the blue 'marriage cup' preserved at the Civico Correr Museum in Venice. This goblet dates from about 1440 and the enamelled portraits of a gentleman and a lady are attributed to the hand of one of the Berovieri, a distinguished family of glassmakers. The

Venetian revival of enamelled glass is often associated with the name of Angelo Beroviero, who, with the help of a well-known Venetian chemist, Paolo Godi da Pergola, perfected the art of colouring the glass metal. Beroviero's son, Marino, is recorded to have been master of the company of 'phiolari' in 1468. Beroviero also had a daughter, Marietta, and an apprentice Giorgio, nicknamed 'Il Ballerino' due to a deformity of his feet. Il Ballerino secretly copied out the recipes for colouring glass and subsequently blackmailed Beroviero for the hand of his daughter. With the added dowry he built his own workshop and founded the glasshouse of Ballerini.

Old Roman methods reappeared with some ingenuity. The heavy, applied ribbing found on bowls and stems of fifteenth-century goblets is a revival of the Roman technique of strengthening glass vessels by rib-moulding. The rediscovery of mixed colour glass, the marbled *'schmelz'* (German *schmelzen* = to melt or fuse) imitating jasper or chalcedony, is attributed to Cristofori Briani and Domenico Miotti, the latter belonging to a well-known glassmaking family. In a surprisingly short period Venetian glassmaking had become an art of highly individual character and only in a small field are we reminded of any Islamic influence, as for instance in the shape of the flared enamelled beaker, popular with Venetian artists for a short period in the fifteenth and early sixteenth century (the Fairfax Cup in the Victoria and Albert Museum). Certain footed ewers with long spouts and trailed and embossed body, and the enamelled pilgrim bottles, are strangely reminiscent of Persian or Byzantine concept and may have been fashioned by foreign craftsmen.

Beads and artificial stones for jewellery were a particular speciality of the early Venetian gaffer. This admiration and love for glittering, brightly coloured stones is also expressed in the enamelling and gilding of early Renaissance vessels. The characteristic gilding of borders in scale-pattern studded with jewel-like drops of coloured enamel, predominantly blue and white, is typical of fifteenth- and early sixteenth-century Venetian glass. The fishscale motif is one frequently found on majolica vessels and it is a decorative pattern that persists in Italian faience ware, such as Deruta, into relatively modern times.

With the *vetro-di-trina*, or lace glass, the Italian gaffer had reached the summit of his achievements. The possible variations of this technique of white enamel threads embedded in a clear glass matrix appear endless, and the fashion lasted well into the seventeenth and eighteenth century. Despite their obvious capability of perfecting the most delicate and ingenious forms of latticinio decoration, the Venetian glassmakers only rarely applied the use of coloured glass threads. Latticinio with threads of red, blue or green intermixed was produced both in the Netherlands and Bohemia and is found in the nineteenth- and twentieth-century reproductions made in Italian workshops. The shapes of latticinio vessels are usually well balanced and of pleasing line. The covered vase or goblet is much favoured by the gaffer and his client and often a further embellishment is added in the form of pineapple moulding at the base of the bowl (plate facing p. 49). Large plates with folded rim, tazzas and footed beakers in lace glass are produced in a style of classical simplicity (plate facing p. 64).

The sensitive relationship between the glassmaker and his material is perhaps best appreciated in the products of the late sixteenth and early seventeenth centuries. The individual character of ice or crackle glass of this period is perfectly expressed in solid, somewhat sculptural forms only occasionally augmented by the application of gilded lion masks. With the increased perfection of Venetian cristallo the character of glass design underwent a sudden transformation. The pedestal stem disappeared almost entirely and was replaced by the hollow baluster which was frequently blown into a lion-mask mould and sprinkled with gold-dust. Enamelling had gone out of fashion during the early sixteenth century due to the fragility of the new glass metal. The colour of cristallo, an exceptionally fluid and easily workable soda glass, was dependent upon its consistency when blown. The thinner the glass bulb, the clearer and 'whiter' the metal. The result was a glass of greater fragility which would not satisfactorily lend itself to the renewed annealing essential for enamelling. A decorative treatment was needed that would rely on the ductility of the metal itself and consequently the entire concept of Venetian glass art changed. The result was the characteristic glass *à la façon de Venise*. Glass design took on an 'upward trend', bowls and stems became taller and more slender, exaggerated flute or trumpet shapes evolved and stems began to gain greater significance. All kinds of imaginative designs were applied to stems, which were hollow blown, mould blown with knops or wrythen decoration or simply balustroid. The fold of the foot or the rim of the bowl, or both, were embellished with an applied trail of colour, usually blue or white (lattimo), a form of decoration already applied in the earlier enamelled vessel of the late fifteenth century. Bowls appeared in fanciful designs, fluted, or flared, of petal shape with crinkled edge. By the late sixteenth century the gaffer became even more adventurous. The plain or dolphin-shaped handles soon adopted most fantastic writhing forms and developed into the *Flügel* or *Schlangenglas* (winged or snaked glass), incorporating latticinio threads of opaque white or sometimes red, embedded in a blue or white glass matrix. The snaked handles themselves were adorned with applied stickered glass or with flattened, pincered blobs. Sometimes the stem itself took the form of some snaked beast supporting the bowl or cup. (Plate facing p. 48.)

The fashion of glass *à la façon de Venise* soon spread. The first emigrant Venetian glassmakers settled in Antwerp during the middle of the sixteenth century, and Liège soon followed suit with glass *à la façon de Venise* produced by enterprising Altarists. Glass made in the Venetian style in the Low Countries is not easily distinguishable from the Venetian product. The blue glass applied is not of such subtle tone as the real Venetian blue, and the white opaque trail and latticinio often has a greyish tinge, when compared with its Venetian counterpart. Enamel twists are frequently mixed red and white, and some of the styles, particularly of glasses from Liège workshops, are less delicate and of more exaggerated design than allowed for by Venetian concept. Crackle glass was extremely well done in Netherland glasshouses. It appears with the applied prunt in the form of Lion masks, the symbol of the Lion of St. Mark's, and also with applied trails of blue around the base and small blue glass or pearl ornaments (plate between pp. 72–73).

Diamond engraving appears in small quantity towards the late sixteenth century. Whereas fused enamel decoration was unpractical for the new cristallo, engraving could be carried out relatively successfully on the soft glass surface, often with additional cold gilding or cold enamelling. Some typical examples of sixteenth-century Venetian diamond engraved glass are found in the work of Jacopo Verzelini, who established his glass-house in London with a monopoly granted in 1575. Verzelini's glasses may be seen in the British Museum and the Victoria and Albert Museum and are usually inscribed or dated, with borders of formal scroll work engraved on the bowls. A typical decorative feature is the lozenge motif, usually found on the base of the bowl and occasionally repeated on the folded foot. The stems are of the hollow blown type, moulded in lion mask or other decorative pattern form (plate facing p. 33). Several glasses in Hall, Tyrol, are of almost identical type both in form and decoration to Verzelini's London-made product, but no satisfactory link-up has yet been explored.

Towards the end of the seventeenth century Venetian glass design became more simplified. Plain, colourless glasses incorporated gadroon-ing on bowls or stems. During the early eighteenth century, due to a flourishing trade with the East, Murano attempted production of opaque white glass, *Milchglas*, in imitation of Chinese porcelain. The Miotti glass-house made milk-glass with attractive enamelling in the European style, such as the set of plates with Venetian views in sepia enamel made for Horace Walpole on his visit to Italy in 1741 (specimen in the British Museum).

The decline of Venetian glass industry and the eventual loss of a mono-poly held over two hundred years was due to a number of coincidental circumstances. Politically and strategically Venice was slowly losing her prominent power. Funds had become drained by continuous wars waged against the Turks, and with the opening of oriental trade routes round the Cape of Good Hope commerce flourished in Spain and the Netherlands. Murano émigrés and Altarists had successfully established a European glass industry which eventually made large glass imports from Venice superfluous. Most decisive of all, Venetian cristallo was superceded by lead or flint glass, a new type of glass developed in England and in Bohemia. A vogue for coloured glass, particularly in the field of interior decorative appliances such as mirrors and chandeliers, continued to be satisfied and supported by the Venetian industry. Glass flowers and plants incorporating bosses and studs of mirror glass were fashionably arranged to create frames for mirrors or to blossom forth on glass chandeliers. The bead industry was still lucrative in 1764 with twenty-two furnaces producing about 44,000 lb. of beads per week. One of the last great mirror-makers, Giuseppe Briati, was so concerned about the downfall of the trade due to competition from Bohemia that he worked for three years in a Bohemian glass factory as a porter. He returned to Murano and was granted a patent to make mirrors and glass by the Bohemian method. Over a hundred years later, in 1866, a company was formed with English capital headed by Dr. Salviati, an Italian lawyer, and Signor Radi, a Murano glassmaker. Many of the old techniques were successfully imitated by this company, renamed after Dr. Salviati's withdrawal the 'Venice and Murano Glass Company'. About seventy pieces of ancient glass from the British Museum collections were copied by this company, including a small cup in the style of the Portland Vase, which took about eight months to engrave. Dr. Salviati concentrated on working in mosaic and a large number of his mosaic pictures were made for English churches and cathedrals, notably Westminster Abbey and St. Paul's.

The Murano workshops of today still manufacture fine glass of original design and colour concept, represented by the workshops of Venini and Ercole Barovier. The monopoly of glass manufacture, however, had passed out of Venetian hands by the beginning of the eighteenth century.

Bohemia and the German-speaking Lands

Czechoslovak glass manufacture embraced the areas of Bohemia, Moravia, Slovakia and Silesia. Bottles and beakers with applied prunts—*Nuppenbecher* (German), with variations that developed into the *Igel* (hedgehog) and the tall *Krautstrunk* (cabbage stalk), were identical to the traditional forms of fifteenth- and sixteenth-century Rhenish glass. The metal produced was the common, greenish waldglas, more or less bubbly and striated, the style remaining popular until the seventeenth century. The evolution of the *Römer* takes place at this later date, with at first the ribbed and later the traditional trailed stem, and bowls engraved in the

Dutch manner. The metal still remains faintly greenish, but is of improved quality and transparency. The 'Angster' or 'Kuttrolf' developed from the antique sprinkler to a popular vessel for holding wines and spirits, with bulbous body and entwined, slightly inclined, long neck. Thin-walled, green drinking beakers developed a high kick, achieved by pushing in the pontil rod at the base and breaking it off so that the glass might stand up more firmly. The kick became more flattened with later date of manufacture, and this applied to many popular vessels such as the *Maigelein*— a small open beaker, the large drinking *Humpen* and the *Passglas*, a tall beaker marked with trailed rings indicating the level to which it had to be emptied by each man as the glass was passed round the company.

During the late fifteenth and sixteenth centuries there was an influx of German glassworkers into Bohemia. Due to the development of the German mining industry the price of fuel began to increase steadily, and small glasshouses often found it more profitable to move to Bohemia and Silesia where conditions were more favourable. In Bohemia alone forty glassworks were extant at the beginning of the sixteenth century and it is claimed that Agricola's knowledge of glassmaking was not only based on information derived from Venetian sources, but also on practical experience gained when the author practised as a doctor in the Bohemian town of Jachymov during the years 1527–33.

Bishoprics and dukedoms, particularly prosperous during the Baroque and Rococo periods, were amply capable and desirous of furthering the production of decorative glassware. The nobility soon realized the advantages of owning large estates in the forest regions and to supplement their income it was quite usual to extend certain privileges to glassmakers and their families. By some strange coincidence the favourite beverages of wine, cider and beer flourished on monastic and ducal soils and the result was the development of suitable drinking vessels of characteristic style. In ecclesiastic life windows for churches, chalices for ritual purposes and receptacles for reliquaries were as essential as the manufacture of beads for rosaries.

Attractive enamelled beakers, goblets, Humpen and Passglasses are associated with Bohemia as well as with the Bavarian and Franconian areas of Nürnberg and Augsburg, and also Tyrol. It is not easy to determine where in the German-speaking countries the fashion began for the Venetian-inspired, and sometimes Venetian-produced, gaily enamelled drinking vessels. A good deal of intermarriage went on in royal circles, and travelling hawkers and glassmakers journeyed to and fro; the art was in this manner influenced by one country and brought to another. Because he left a diary the best-known of these travelling glass salesmen was George Francis Kreybich, a Czech from Kamenicky Senov, who started off as an apprentice glass painter and engraver. Accompanied by a relative, Kreybich set out with a wheelbarrow full of glassware and his engraving equipment. During the years 1683 to 1721 he undertook thirty journeys, including visits to Russia, Poland, Hungary, Germany, Turkey, Italy, England, Denmark and Sweden. He arrived in London in 1688, almost shipwrecked, and wrote that business was poor during the first few weeks because there were already six glassworks existing in the city at that time. He also explained that "our glass was painted and there is nothing similar on the market as yet". The enterprising Kreybich managed an introduction to the Court and in consequence sold every piece of his glass. He returned after witnessing James's abdication and possibly left behind some inspiration for the engraved and enamelled glass that became popular in England during the eighteenth century.

German and Bohemian enamelling gained popularity in the latter half of the sixteenth century, and alongside a taste for cut and engraved glass it remained in fashion well into the eighteenth century. From 1570–91 a glasshouse was in operation in Innsbruck under royal patronage.

Decorative subjects were usually connected with the domestic and industrial life of the burghers and their regents. A frequent motif is the double-headed eagle, the *Reichsadler* (Imperial Eagle), and this is supplemented by scenes of important events in the life of the reigning duke or monarch. Despite their elevated status, figural representations are charmingly naïve and refreshing and Biblical scenes and ecclesiastic emblems have the same naturalistic approach (frontispiece). A popular theme is the 'seven ages of man', and arms of heraldry and guilds are

Bohemian or Silesian twelve-sided colourless glass bottle, the bottom cut in a roundel with radiating rays. Painted in red with Chinese figures and floral and animal motifs in the Rococo manner. Attributed to Ignatz Preissler, *c.* 1730. Ht. 13·3 cm.

18th-century sealed wine bottles, *left to right*, greenish brown glass, impressed with the seal 'P. Bastard 1725'. Ht. 18 cm.; impressed 'W. Bastard 1753'. Ht. 26 cm.; a brown bottle impressed 'Polloxfen Basturo 1730'. Ht. 19 cm.

Newcastle-upon-Tyne goblet, enamelled in colour with the Royal Arms of England, flanked by the thistle and rose. Rococo motifs in puce and white. The reverse of the bowl bears the Prince of Wales' plumes and motto. Enamelling by a member of the Beilby family; c. 1762. Ht. 22 cm.

Spanish decanter-jug of colourless glass, the neck and body decorated by wheel-engraving and gilding. One side shows a bird, the other a hare. From the factory of La Granja de San Ildefonso, near Segovia, c. 1775–80. Ht. 30·5 cm.

found in great variety. Pewter-mounted and handled beer-mugs with profuse decorative detail appear to have been greatly favoured in mid-seventeenth-century Bohemia and were often made of a particularly attractive cobalt-blue glass. Enamelled glasses from these regions are usually dated and often inscribed with the name of the owner or donor, so that there is little difficulty in dating and placing the vessel. Certain areas are associated with a distinctive pictorial type of enamelling, as for instance the 'Ochsenkopf' Humpen made in the glass-houses of the Fichtelgebirge, so called after its second highest mountain. In this case the usual decorative theme illustrates mountainous landscapes and animals of the forest with the obvious symbol of the oxen head with the three rivers (Eger, Elbe, Saale) springing from the mountain. Saxonia, too, was proficient in enamelling. The small, 3- to 4-in. beakers decorated with heraldic emblems in bright colours are attributed to this area, as are also the early-eighteenth-century Passglasses with their delightful enamelled representations of playing-cards. A further identifiable vessel is the Hallorenglas, a tall beaker illustrating motifs connected with the 'Salzpfännerschaft' (The Salters' Guild), produced in Halle, on the River Saale. (Plate between pp. 72–73.)

A far more sophisticated result was achieved by the enamelling tech-niques of Johann Schaper (1621–70) working in Nürnberg and Ignaz Preissler (c. 1675–1733) who was employed, together with his son, on the estate of the wealthy Bohemian landowner, Count Kolovrat. Schaper's methods were derived from his experience in the art of stained glass and the delicate enamelling of his landscapes and figures was almost exclusively carried out in the medium of Schwarzlot. His black or sepia enamelling is usually found on the so-called 'Schaper Glass', a cylindrical beaker stand-ing on three flattened ball feet (plate facing p. 72). Preissler augmented his Schwarzlot with red enamel and gilding. His style is typical of Rococo taste with garlands and foliage, and gay little vignettes of hunting scenes. Following the general trend, chinoiserie motifs are also found in Preissler's decorative enamelling (plate facing p. 80).

Bohemia's great contribution to art glass development lies in the field of cutting and engraving. The revival of this art is associated with Caspar

Lehman (1570–1622), lapidary to the Court of Rudolf II at Prague. At that time vessels of Bohemian rock crystal (*böhmisches Bergkristall*) in elegant shapes, competently carved, were in great demand. Expensively mounted and set with precious stones they recalled a fashion popular in the Renaissance Italy of Cellini. The supply of rock crystal, however, was not inexhaustible and mining was costly. It was Lehman's practical idea to transfer rock crystal cutting techniques to objects made of glass. The art of cutting and engraving glass had been lost for some centuries, because the fashionable Venetian cristallo was quite unsuitable for this treatment. The Bohemian development of a robust potash-lime glass which lent itself to carving did not take place until about 1670, and the achievement of Lehman and his followers with the medium of soda glass is a remarkable one. It is assumed that the first work produced by Lehman was the engraving of glass panels in matt, shallow cut with occasional use of diamond point. The 'Perseus and Andromeda' panel at the Victoria and Albert Museum is attributed to Lehman's hand, and an armorial beaker signed and dated 1605 at the Industrial Art Museum in Prague shows allegorical figures in the same type of broad, stylized treatment. The monopoly granted to Lehman in 1609 for the application of glass engraving was inherited on his death by a gifted pupil, George Schwanhardt (1601–67). Schwanhardt settled in Nürnberg during the strife of the Thirty Years' War, one of his innovations being to give a bright polish to some of the engraved parts, resulting in a more realistic and lively representation. Schwanhardt, with his sons George and Henry, founded a distinctive school of glass cutting. Henry is credited with the discovery of etching by fluoric acid, an accidental event due to a drop of the fluid ruining his spectacles. In the manner of the master, the Schwanhardts used the lapidary's wheel for cutting and the diamond for engraving their glasses. In Dresden, Lehman's art was carried on by another pupil, Caspar Schindler. Among his followers most active in Nürnberg were H. W. Schmidt and in particular Hermann Schwinger (1640–83), who was exceptionally skilful in the delicate treatment of naturalistic scenes. The typical Nürnberg vessel of this time is represented by the *Deckelpokal*, a tall, covered goblet of relatively thin metal with either a hollow inverted baluster, a knopped stem, or a stem incorporating both features, interspersed by numerous pairs of mereses (flat collars) and an extravagantly formed finial to the cover. One of the last of the great Nürnberg engravers, Georg Friedrich Killinger, died in 1726. His work is characterized by an exceptionally advanced conception of realistic pictorial representation. Work by these artists is often signed and can, therefore, be easily identified (plate facing p. 72).

About the year 1700 Bohemian glass cutters received a new impetus in the form of waterpower applied for driving the cutter's lathes. The *Radzieher*, the assistant who turned the wheel of the engraver's lathe by means of a thong and handle, was an indispensable member of the glass engraver's workshop. Schwanhardt was helped in this task by members of his own family. The method of mechanization allowed a new freedom for the cutter and his work resulting in a revival in the manner of rock crystal engraving. Heavy cutting and stylized scrollwork decoration in high relief was made possible by the perfection of the more resistant potash-lime glass. A thicker-walled vessel became essential, assuming a more massive and perhaps a little less elegant shape, with shorter, thicker stems and simplified finial decoration.

The best engraved glass was made during the early part of the eighteenth century in Silesia, where wheel engraving was of exceptionally high standard. The hollow and/or knopped stem with mereses, typical for the later seventeenth century, was replaced by the solid, cut stem soon after the year 1700. The so-called 'Silesian stem', a four-sided (later more numerous-sided or faceted) solid stem descending from a squarish-cut shoulder knop and tapering towards the foot, was not confined to Silesian glass alone, but was manufactured in various other regions such as Bohemia, Bavaria and Prussia. It was probably introduced into England with some German glass exported to London in 1709. (This could not be auctioned because of a boycott led by the local glass industry.) Both *Hoch-* and *Tief-schnitt* (intaglio) were actively employed, and by the mid-eighteenth century Rococo charm is typified in the pastoral scenes and the *Laub und Bandelwerk*, a design of scrolls and garlands replacing the heavier acanthus leaf motifs.

The enamel twist makes its appearance in Bohemian glass of the later eighteenth century. It takes the form not so much of a white, but of a mixed colour twist, with a preference for red.

Several German glasshouses produced cut and engraved vessels not easily distinguishable from Bohemian glass. The Lauensteiner Hütte, founded about 1700, was supposedly the first factory to have applied the Ravenscroft formula for lead glass. Unfortunately their process was not entirely successful, most Lauensteiner glass being affected by crizzling, the glass disease so typical of Ravenscroft's early attempts. The same misfortune befell the earlier products of glasshouses such as Potsdam and Kassel. Glasses that can definitely be identified with Lauenstein manufacture are those pieces signed under the base with a lion rampant—for Lauenstein (Löwenstein)—and the cipher 'C' standing for Calenberg, the district in which the factory was situated. In order to apply this trade mark the pontil mark was ground away and this conditioned frequently a distinctive, domed foot.

The Kassel glasshouse must be mentioned for its association with one of the most distinguished and able glass-engravers of the early eighteenth century, Franz Gondelach (born in 1663) who, like Lehman in Prague, was elevated to be *Fürstlicher Glasschneider* to the Landgrave Karl of Hessen-Kassel. Gondelach worked in both *Hoch-* and *Tiefschnitt* techniques and used the diamond for particularly fine design. He was an extremely versatile artist who also engraved and cut rock crystal. Pastoral and allegorical scenes are represented with almost plastic effect and among the portrait busts carved in high relief Gondelach included also the likeness of his Landgrave. An eight-pointed star design under the base is found on several specimens attributed to Gondelach.

Two of the most capable engravers associated with the Potsdam glass factory were Gottfried Spiller and Martin Winter (d. 1702). Spiller (d. 1721) was Gondelach's teacher and is best known for his excellent intaglio cutting and the superb engraving of his favourite subject, the human body. Potsdam glasses were both cut and engraved in the Silesian and Bohemian tradition but with the additional decoration of gilding. Coloured cut glass of a deep blue and emerald green are also typical products of this factory.

The most interesting development at Potsdam was achieved by Johann Kunckel (1630–1703) with his *Goldrubinglas*, the gold-ruby glass. The Potsdam glass factory was founded in 1674 by the Elector Frederick William of Brandenburg. One of his first acts was to employ Kunckel as chief chemist and he remained with the Potsdam factory for twenty years. Sometime before 1679 he developed a beautiful deep-red glass which was particularly effective by transmitted light. The glass colour was perfected by the addition of gold, obtained by the usual method of melting down golden ducats, and reheating the glass after completion, a technique that was instrumental in intensifying the desired colour. Although Kunckel tried to maintain the secrecy of his process, gold-ruby glass found several imitators who achieved a similar effect by adding copper to the glass batch instead of the expensive precious metal. Kunckel glasses are mainly of classical form with plain facet cutting without the addition of pictorial embellishment. Ruby glass decorated by engraving of ornamental or pictorial character with motifs of fruit and vines is usually of South German manufacture, particularly when set in attractive metal mounts.

The successor of Kunckel's protector, who was later to become Frederick I, showed no great sympathy for the efforts and achievements of his chief chemist. He demanded an account of all expenses involved in Kunckel's experiments. As was to be expected, the precious materials necessary, and the frequent failures which are unavoidable in any kind of research, added up to a considerable amount. Frederick asked for repayment of the debts incurred but the required sum exceeded by far Kunckel's modest pocket and he was obliged to sell his house to meet this unreasonable demand. It was a sadly undeserved fate for such an able and dedicated scientist, who died in 1703, a disillusioned man.

It might be useful to mention at this point a gifted Thuringian glass engraver, G. E. Kunckel (not to be confused with the Potsdam chemist), who was active during the earlier half of the eighteenth century. Kunckel's highly accomplished work, usually found on tall covered goblets, is comparable with the fine work of Jacob Sang, the Saxon engraver who settled in Amsterdam about 1753.

The revival of Zwischengold glass techniques was forecast in Johann

Kunckel's work *Ars Vitraria Experimentalis* (1678) but the method was successfully re-applied in Bohemian workshops during the period 1720–45. Zwischengold decoration is mainly found on faceted beakers and less frequently on tall goblets. The goldfoil which is enclosed between the two beakers is engraved with a fine needle and the design is occasionally highlighted by coloured lacquer, predominantly red and green, in the manner of *verre églomisée*. A rare variation of the double-walled beaker was produced in Bohemia about 1690–1720, whereby the gold foil covered the entire surface of the inner vessel. The inner surface of the outer beaker is enamelled in colours recalling the marbled effect of Venetian agate or chalcedony glass. As mentioned earlier, these rare double-walled vessels have the joint at the top of the rim. The later Zwischengold beakers are decorated with hunting or pastoral scenes, and also on occasion with monastic emblems. The inner beaker overlaps the outer vessel and the joint shows about 1 cm. below the rim. (Pl. facing p. 128.)

A further elaboration of the Zwischengold technique was developed by Joseph Mildner (1763–1808), working at Gutenbrunn in Austria. The method of decoration mostly associated with this able and versatile artist consists of miniature portrait panels and medallions fitted in the wall of the glass, which has been hollowed out accordingly. Mildner decorated porcelain as well as parchment and one of his techniques was to enclose the parchment miniature in the glass matrix. The reverse side of the painting was usually signed by the artist and included the name of the sitter, the date and perhaps a motto or dedication. From the late eighteenth century onward, ornamentation assumes a more intimate character and the romanticism of nineteenth-century Biedermeier heralds the sentimental aspect of the Victorian age. Family and historical portraits, dedications and protestations of fidelity, views of cities and famous buildings are remembered for ever on their glassy back-cloth.

Exquisite glass decoration in the form of transparent enamels was the specialized work of Samuel Mohn (1762–1815) of Dresden. This delicate enamelling presents a direct contrast to the work of an earlier Dresden artist, the court enameller Johann Friedrich Meyer (1680–1752), who worked in a distinctive raised enamel technique. Mohn's son, Gottlob

86

Samuel (1789–1825), settled in Vienna, where his technique greatly influenced the more prolific Anton Kothgasser (1769–1851). Skilfully executed views of buildings and figurative subjects are usually framed in a cartouche of gilding. The most popular vessel for this type of enamelling is the plain, flared beaker of transparent white or yellow stained glass, with cut 'cogwheel' base. Glasses by the Mohns, who also painted silhouettes, are relatively rare, but the work of Kothgasser and some of his imitators such as Hoffmeister of Vienna and Carl V. Scheidt of Berlin have appeared recently in the auction-rooms.

The first half of the nineteenth century witnessed some fascinating developments in the manufacture of Bohemian coloured glass. Ultramarine blue, which effects tone changes from the palest to almost black, was developed and consequently applied to glass from 1826 onward. At the beginning of the nineteenth century green was considered an unfashionable colour and not manufactured in quantity. By the 1830s, however, it regained popularity following the introduction of Josef Riedel's *Annagrün* and *Annagelb*. Riedel, of Dolny Polubny in Northern Bohemia, obtained these colours by adding small quantities of uranium and vitriol to his batch. Named after Riedel's wife Anna Maria Riedel, *Annagrün* and *Annagelb* glass is of a transparent, fluorescent, green to yellow metal. It was usually improved by cutting and gilding and was rarely produced after 1848.

An attractive stained-glass technique confined to yellow and red and applied to ornamental glass was produced by silver and copper stain. The popularity of this technique is attributed to the work of the chemist Bedrich Egerman of Novy Bor. Egerman had experimented with and accomplished this technique during the years 1815–25 but the secrets of the process were stolen and the method was applied in neighbouring glassworks. More familiar is another ingenious invention of Egerman's, the 'Lythyalin' glass, a polished opaque or translucent multi-coloured glass, akin to the Venetian 'Schmelz' or marbled glass and first exhibited in Prague in 1829 (plate facing p. 88). Another 'stone' glass was developed a little earlier in the glassworks of Count Buquoy, Georg Franz August Longueval, in southern Bohemia. Contrary to some conceptions Buquoy's 'Hyalith' glass is always an entirely black, non-transparent glass, of exceptional fragility with poor heat resistance. The applied decoration consisted mostly of fired gilding. A monopoly of manufacture was granted to the Count in 1820. The secret of Hyalith glass died with its inventor and the recipe was re-discovered among the Count's papers only a few years ago, just over a hundred years after his death. Buquoy also manufactured glass of opaque colours such as solid blues and reds.

Milky white and coloured alabaster glass was manufactured in profusion during the later nineteenth century, as was also the overlay glass with its glittering opaque white produced by the addition of stannic oxide. Carved and gilded, painted with flowers and portraits, adorned with glass-drops and pewter mounts, it was a case of workmanship outstripping taste and refinement. Coloured and gilded glass of the later Victorian period, with applied portrait and flower medallions, is not easily distinguishable from the Stourbridge product of the same period. Engraving, however, was always of brilliant quality in Bohemian glass and the mid-nineteenth century produced excellent engraved work on overlay and flashed glass, the latter being produced by the staining process. A variety of engraved subjects and portraits are found on glasses of this period. One of the best artists specializing in portraits was Dominic Biman, active during the first half of the nineteenth century. K. Pfohl, working in the second half of the century, in Kamecky Senov, seems to have concentrated on spirited engravings of horses and his work is easily recognizable. (Pl. facing p. 129.) Bohemia has always been one of the largest producers of beads and chandeliers. Experience and superior quality of cutting has made this country the leading supplier of cut-glass chandeliers.

The *art nouveau* or *Jugendstil* movement inspired a great artistic response from the glass industry. Louis Lobmeyr, of Vienna, a glass designer and industrialist, brought together some of the best Austrian and Czech artists with the aim of making glass, not by mass production but on an individually inspired artistic level. Exploitation of ancient techniques coupled with advanced scientific approach makes this period one of the most exciting in the history of ornamental glass. Accent was on colour and iridescence. Tiffany's success in America inspired a glass development on similar lines in Bohemian factories such as Moser at Nove Dvory and

88

Left to right, thick, opaque-white, pressed beaker by Sowerby. The motif in relief represents schoolboys on their bench. Such exceptional colour treatment on Sowerby's glass is unusual; *c*. 1845–50. Ht. 10 cm.; white opaline beaker with rococo motifs applied in gilding. Bohemian, *c*. 1820. Ht. 8·5 cm.; scent bottle by Egerman (Bohemia) in typical red Lythialin glass, *c*. 1830. Ht. 7·5 cm.

Lötz Witwe at Klostermühle. In Berlin, Koepping's elegant and brittle glasses combined individual style with impractical design and inadequate technical quality. The most successful iridescent glass style was perhaps that of the Lötz factory, with interesting colour fluctuations and a more purposeful design than Tiffany's originals. A general trend of adding the maker's name and/or the artist's signature to the completed piece is a great encouragement to the collector of art nouveau glass.

Netherlandish Glass

The glass style evolved in Holland and Belgium is the result of an industry based on foreign inspiration. In the technique of diamond engraving, Dutch artists were among the first and most respected in the field. Eighteenth-century Netherland must be credited with the artistic perfection of a glass-engraving technique which was accomplished nowhere else and is as peculiarly Dutch as the interiors of Pieter de Hooch or a still-life by de Heem a hundred years earlier.

Fourteenth- and fifteenth-century glassmakers working in the areas of the Rhineland and the Lorraine were well placed for distributing their products, or even moving on themselves by way of convenient river transport toward the lowlands. The influence of these early glaziers was never entirely removed from Netherland glass conception. The glass metal itself was the greenish or brownish *verre de fougère* or *Waldglas*, which inspired the preference for a delicately tinted green-coloured glass, popular for several centuries. The glass blobs or prunts of the Rhenish beaker became more sophisticated and by the seventeenth century the raspberry prunt typified an accepted form of ornament, in particular for that most popular of Rhenish drinking glasses, the Roemer. The evolution of the beaker with applied prunts to the Roemer of distinctive shape was a slow process of some hundred to a hundred and fifty years, and even in its most sophisticated form the vessel was given a deliberate green or greenish-blue tinge. The wine-bottle had grown 'upwards' during its evolution; from the round or square keg of antiquity through the bulbous phase with at first the short and later the longer neck, until, by the eighteenth century, it assumed the form we know today. The Roemer, on the other hand, evolved its shape by growing 'downward'; the prunted beaker grew a small flat, and sometimes trailed, foot, which developed into the hollow stem with applied raspberry prunts and a spreading foot made of spirally wound glass. The bowl assumed a globular form and the prunt decoration became confined to the stem. A Roemer at the Victoria and Albert Museum with applied prunts in the form of lions' masks serves as a stimulating example of two of the main influences in Dutch and Flemish glassmaking—the Rhenish and the Venetian.

Venetian glass was first made at Antwerp during the middle of the sixteenth century, although it seems probable that Venetian or Altarist craftsmen were employed in Netherland glass industry before 1550. On April 1st, 1549, a reluctant prince from Spain came to meet his father, the Emperor Charles V, in the city of Brussels. The twenty-two-year-old Philip was to remain at his father's side for three years in order to become acquainted with the dominions that would one day be his to rule. In the autumn of 1549 father and son visited the glasshouse at Beauwelz, and documents relating to the visit refer to gifts of glass made to the royal guests. An enormous glass ship, 50 in. long, applied with lion mask prunts and decorated with glass figures of sailors and animals, was certainly of Venetian workmanship and follows the pattern of the ship, or 'nef', fashionable as a table centre-piece. Glass ships were favourite diversions of the glassblower's skill and often fulfilled the function of wine containers at the Venetian table. The ship, as well as other glass objects offered to the prince, were not made of soda glass, but of "greenish glass in the manner of German glass", obviously the common *Waldglas*. It may be assumed, therefore, that although glass was made in the Venetian style either by local or foreign craftsmen there was no successful production of cristallo glass until the latter half of the sixteenth century. Glass *à la façon de Venise* had become fashionable throughout Europe by the beginning of the seventeenth century and nowhere was it so avidly copied as in the Netherlands workshops, particularly at Liège (plate facing p. 48). A good latticinio, also from Liège, was most likely produced by Italian glassworkers and flute glasses were made both in plain and latticinio techniques. The form of the flute seems Venetian in origin, although there is a variety appearing to be a cross between the flute and the *Passglas*, with applied milled rings. Flutes were in the first instance meant to hold wine but by the later seventeenth century champagne and ale were drunk from this vessel. A famous group of glasses comprising the 'Chesterfield' and 'Exeter' flutes, engraved with ciphers and arms of the owners or with subjects of historical significance, were most certainly decorated by Dutch artists. A light brownish soda metal and folded foot are common to all the famous engraved flutes. Although they are generally considered to be of English manufacture, the flat foot and colour of the metal leave some doubt as to whether they are not a Netherlands import.

The still-life painting of the Dutch and Flemish schools is a faithful indicator of the type of glass in domestic use. The Venetian-style tazza and covered goblet, the wineglass with spiky or flammiform gadrooning of the bowl, the elegant flute and the distinctive Roemer enjoyed equal popularity during the seventeenth and early eighteenth centuries. A type of giant Roemer with tall or short stem often formed the centrepiece of a well-furnished table as a prized family possession.

The Dutch skill of engraving resulted in much of this work being done to order. By the latter half of the seventeenth century wheel engraving supplemented the diamond point technique. The somewhat stiff portraits, as for instance the head of Charles II appearing on several historical flutes and goblets, give way to a far more interesting style of decoration. Allegorical scenes and grotesque figures in the manner of Jacques Callot, the most able of all French graphic artists, were transmitted on glass by engravers such as Carel du Quesne in a fluency of style hitherto not possible. Cipher or calligraphic glasses fall into a special category; here again we must admire the accomplishment of the engraver and his treatment of the fragile material. Graceful swirls and flourishes in the manner of illuminated manuscripts were highly prized, many of the large communities having their own skilled semi-official calligrapher.

Anna Roemers Visscher (1583–1651), of Amsterdam, is the earliest of the calligraphic engravers we know of, since she signed most of her diamond-engraved glasses. In this ornamental glass style, swirls and flourishes are woven into an intricate pattern covering the entire surface of the glass bowl, representing generally some encouraging motto or proverb. In the manner of still-life painters Anna Roemers Visscher introduced fruit, insect and plant-forms into the calligraphic design. One of her glasses dated 1646 incorporates a stipple-engraved cherry, some seventy or eighty years ahead of the fashion. Most of the work of this gifted artist is found on the Roemer style glass of generous proportion, often 14 to 15 in. high, designed as a gift of friendship and accordingly inscribed. Maria Tessel-schade Roemers Visscher (1595–1649), Anna's sister, and Anna Maria van Schurman (1607–78), both produced work in similar style. A little later, Adam and Willem Jakobsz engraved calligraphic glasses in Leyden. Heemskerk, a cloth merchant who wrote poetry, was a more enterprising glass engraver. He applied his calligraphic designs also to Venetian-style baluster glasses and occasionally introduced wheel engraving in his work (plate facing p. 48).

Diamond engraving of the Italianate, hatched technique, representing foliage and fruiting vines, was applied in particular to bulbous bottles or decanters of transparent white and coloured glass. A light bottle-green, transparent glass was quite common; a blue is also occasionally found and is exceptionally attractive. The name of Willem Moleyser is often asso-ciated with diamond engraving of this type and with the motifs of fruiting vines and dancing peasants. Many of the Dutch engravers were well-to-do amateurs and proud enough of their achievements to sign their work. The monogram 'CFM' is that of the Hague glass engraver Christoffel Jsz. Meyer, who seems to have had a preference for engraving tall flutes with allegorical subjects. Two of his glasses in the collection of the late A. J. Guepin, Eindhoven, are dated 1662. An amateur artist and flax merchant, Marinus Hendriksz van Gelder was working at about the same period in Rotterdam, and he signed his glasses either in full or with the initials M.v.G.

An entirely new character was given to Dutch glass engraving by the invention of carrying out the design entirely in diamond stippling. Frans Greenwood (1680–1761), of English ancestry and living in Dordrecht, is credited with the first application of this technique. The technique itself, coupled with closer-linked political ties, brought a new element to Netherlands glass development in the fashion for glasses '*à l'Angleterre*'. English glasses in the Netherlandish style were ordered by Greenwood from the Newcastle glasshouse of Dagnia, an Altarist family brought to England by Mansell. The thousands of tiny dots or minute lines making up a stipple-engraved design were applied either with the diamond point or with a steel needle fitted into a hammer. The brilliance of English lead glass, in particular the whiteness of the Newcastle product, and the softness of its metal combine to make Dutch diamond stippling one of the finest artistic achievements in glass decoration. With the improvement of the metal Greenwood's technique improved also. His subjects range from flowers and fruit to portraits and figures of great vitality, and here again we find designs based on characters created by Callot, especially on the Commedia del' Arte. The possibility of denser stippling enhanced the refractive properties of the metal and enabled a more brilliant contrast of light and shade.

Greenwood's signatures vary from the full name to mere initials. One of his earliest signed glasses, a drawn trumpet with line engraving, is dated 1720 and may be seen at the Victoria and Albert Museum.

The technique of stippling was carried out successfully by a number of Dutch engravers, some of whom are known by their signed work. Art Schouman, a colleague, and G. H. Hoolaart, signing 'GHH', supposedly a nephew of Greenwood, are among some of the better-known stipple engravers. Another engraver employing this technique signs his work J. van den Blinjk, and he and his better-known colleagues are represented in the larger museum collections.

The greatest number of stippled glasses are attributed to the hand of a later artist, David Wolff (1732–98), although at present we know of the existence of only ten or so signed glasses, all dated between the years 1784–96. Charming putty among clouds in various allegorical attitudes and children in delightfully formal dress are generally associated with Wolff's glasses. This artist was extremely versatile and his subjects include commemorative as well as portrait glasses of exceptional artistic ability, which may well support the assumption that he was a trained painter. Although attempts were made at lead glass production in the Netherlands, most stipple-engraved glasses were of English manufacture. Wolff seems to have favoured two distinct types; the typical Newcastle glass of the later eighteenth century distinguished by the flared bowl and tall stem, composed of two knops containing double rows of tears above two opposed balusters, and the glass with ovoid bowl and faceted stem which may have been cut in Holland (plate facing p. 96).

Wheel engraving was produced in the Netherlands on an exceptionally high level. One of the finest glass engravers, a contemporary of Wolff, was Jacob Sang, who called himself a 'Saxon artist-glass-engraver'. His earliest signature is found on a marriage goblet of 1737. In 1753 he advertised in the Amsterdam *Courant* that he would cut and engrave on "English goblets, panes, cabinet panels and boxlids the most fashionable curiosities known and practised in Holland, whether in large or small figures, perspective or relief, shallow or deep-cut on matt or rough grounds, polished figures, coats-of-arms, names in any type of script, portraits, rock- and scroll-work of the newest fashion, Ovidian or other stories. . . ." An example of Sang's engraving is found on a representative English lead glass of about 1700, in the British Museum. This is a covered goblet 19½ in. high with a figure-of-eight stem with pincered frills, the bowl and domed cover partly decorated in 'nipped diamond waies' with a finial repeating the design of the stem. The bowl shows an exemplary engraving of the ship *Velzen* and the reverse side is inscribed with a commemorative address in poem form. It is signed and dated 1757 and one hopes that this commission may have been the result of one of Sang's copious advertisements. A distinct Germanic flavour can be detected in some of Sang's exacting work and most certainly his training was derived from workshops in his native Saxony.

During the eighteenth century, manufacture of lead glass was attempted in the towns of Ghent, Namur, Liège, Middleburgh and s'Hertogenbosch, Wolff's birthplace. As early as 1680 the Bonhomme factory at Liège engaged workmen to make glass *à la façon d'Angleterre*. Some good English-style wineglasses were made at Liège in the mid-eighteenth century. During the first half of the century bowls of drinking glasses show a variety of mould-blown decorations, in particular small indentations such as beechnut moulding and also honeycomb moulding. Stems are rib-

94

twisted and the domed or conical feet are quite similar in character to English glasses of the same period. The lead content, however, is smaller than in English glass and consequently the foreign product is lighter in weight. The same observation may be applied to interior enamel twists produced at Liège in the later eighteenth century. The identical design was also manufactured in a soda glass metal and can scarcely be confused with the good-quality contemporary English enamel twist.

Despite a progressively developing lead glass production in the Netherlands, Dutch engravers preferred glasses of English origin. The softness, weight and colour of the metal, together with the well-proportioned baluster shape, make the Newcastle product unmistakable.

In 1765 a new factory was established at Leerdam, near Rotterdam, the Royal Dutch Glassworks. Ornamental glass and tableware were produced on the same lines as contemporary German- and French-designed glass, the French influence being particularly noticeable during the art nouveau period. The factory still flourishes today.

The British Isles

Much literature is available on the various aspects of English glass to stimulate and encourage the student and the collector who wishes to specialize. From the technical point of view England's great merit lies in the development of a glass of lead which was superior in all respects to glass made elsewhere at the time. From the collector's point of view the English glasshouse was instrumental in supplying one of the most fascinating and desirable objects—the eighteenth-century drinking glass.

One of the earliest settlements of glaziers occurred about 1226, or even before, in the Chiddingfold district of the Weald. Glassmakers from Normandy preferred the well-wooded areas of the Weald of Surrey, Sussex and Kent and they were joined in their craft by families from the Lorraine. When the fuel supply became exhausted they moved from one region to the next, to Gloucestershire and Staffordshire, where in the mid-sixteenth century the Tyzacks (du Thisacs), Henzeys (de Hennezel), Titterys (de Thietry) and Hoes (de Houx) became the fathers of the Stourbridge glass industry.

Glass originating from the Weald areas is commonly referred to as 'Wealden' glass and the little we know of it is from finds made in the form of fragments near old glasshouse sites. In common with European glass of this early period beakers and bottles are of the greenish or yellowish metal associated with Waldglas, but not comparable in quality with the Continental product. The chief industry was the manufacture of window-glass, even though the best white and coloured glass was imported for this purpose, mainly from France. With the waning of Roman influence, Anglo-Saxon claw-beakers, delicate cone beakers and drinking horns of simple form with spiral trails may well have been 'British made'. We know that John le Alemayne, who supplied window-glass to St. Stephen's Chapel in Westminster about 1350–57, also sold "cuppis to drink", but glassware for the royal table was a luxury import from Venice. The real beginning of English glassmaking history came in 1567, when the Lorrainer Jean Carré obtained a licence to manufacture glass for glazing by the method used in Burgundy and Lorraine. The enterprising Carré, who had come to England by way of Antwerp, joined the Wealden glass industry and was instrumental in bringing over the families of Tyzack, Henzey, Tittery and Hoe mentioned earlier. He was furthermore granted a licence to manufacture in London glass *à la façon de Venise*, and it was to take charge of Carré's Crutched Friars glasshouse that Giacomo (Jacopo) Verzelini (1522–1606) arrived in 1571 from Venice. About a year after the arrival of this most able of Venetian glassmakers Carré died, and for the next twenty years glass *à la façon de Venise* was manufactured at Crutched Friars and several other glasshouses under the supervision of the purposeful Verzelini. Undaunted by the manipulations of jealous glass merchants and importers, Verzelini applied for, and was granted by the Sovereign Elizabeth I, the sole English right to manufacture glass *à la façon de Venise* for twenty-one years. Thus encouraged, the Venetian promptly took out naturalization papers.

About nine of the dozen or so glasses associated with Verzelini manufacture can definitely be attributed to his London glasshouse. The earliest of these, dated 1577, is in the Corning (N.Y.) Museum of Glass and several others are in English museums. Most of Verzelini's work incorporates the

Norwegian goblet made at the factory of Nøstetangen. Wheel-engraving on bowl, showing a glasshouse with men working at the furnace and annealing ovens, executed by Heinrich Köhler in 1770. Ht. 18 cm.

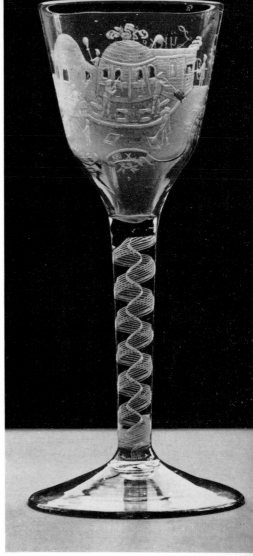

A colourless glass presentation goblet, probably from Newcastle-upon-Tyne. Dutch stipple engraving attributed to David Wolff, 1791. Cutting extends to the base of the bowl, creating the effect of a many-petalled flower. Reverse side of the bowl is inscribed with verses, the foot with a dedication in honour of the K.W.D.A.V. Society's 25th anniversary, both in diamond point. Ht. 18·5 cm.

A Baccarat dark-blue weight, having two entwined trefoil garlands of red and white canes around a central butterfly cane with animal silhouettes, enclosed by a double overlay of dark blue over opaque white, and star-cut base; c. 1848. Dia. 8·2 cm.

Opaque white vase made in South Staffordshire in the Chinese style, enamelled in colours with figures; a bird among plants on the reverse side. A gilt border is applied around the neck; c. 1770. Ht. 17·5 cm.

Venetian hollow, mould-blown knop (or bulb) in the stem, and bowls are of ample proportion. Diamond point engraving in the hatched, Italian fashion, is attributed to the hand of Anthony de Lisle, who came from the 'Dominions of the King of France' and applied for citizenship in 1597. Stylized scrolls or floral sections and lozenge motifs which may also be found on the foot of the vessel, are typical of his work. Dates, names and inscriptions, and friezes of stags and hounds often encircle the cup, and enamelled or gilded decoration is applied only in rare instances. The particularly soft, faintly greenish hue of Verzelini's soda metal imbues his glasses with a kind of remote tranquillity, which is quite striking (plate facing p. 33).

With Verzelini began the era of monopolies. He retired in 1592 and into his shoes stepped an old soldier, Sir Jerome Bowes, who extended the monopoly and continued to manufacture glass in Verzelini's style at his Broad Street glasshouse until 1604, after which date the licence was sold from one profiteer to another. On May 23rd, 1615, came the famous 'proclamation touching glasses' and the subsequent utilization of coal. On May 22nd, 1623, a patent was granted to Sir Robert Mansell (1573–1656), a retired admiral, to "use exercise practise sett up and putt in use the arte feate and misterie" of making all kinds of glassware with any kind of "fewell whatsoever not being tymber or wood". The 1615 Edict was a boon to someone of Mansell's farsightedness and industrial ability, and the development of the coal-mining industry, both in his native Wales and on the Tyneside, began with this enterprising personality. In 1630 the famous Dagnia glassmaking family settled in Newcastle, and soon Mansell's empire embraced Scotland, Staffordshire, Swansea, King's Lynn, London and Purbeck Island. For the first time glass manufacture was organized on an industrial scale, although Mansell knew little enough about glass himself and had to rely on foreign workmen. Frequent clashes with these imported artisans, and the difficulties created by the Scots, who would entice away workmen as soon as they had been trained, and also refused to supply coal, brought bitter disappointments to Mansell's endeavours. He is said to have lost a personal fortune of some £30,000 before the industry was successfully established. Industrial sabotage included deliberately poor workmanship and the output was consequently of variable quality. Fragments and glasses assigned to Mansell's glasshouse show an Italian- and Netherlands-inspired product, with the softness and sparkle of Venetian cristallo but of thicker blown metal. A Venetian, Antonio Miotti, who worked at the time at Middleburgh in the Netherlands, was brought over to take charge of the London glasshouse, and no doubt good-quality glass *à la façon de Venise* was made there. Cylindrical beer glasses with trailed rings in the manner of the German Passglas or incorporating latticinio stripes were exported by Mansell in great quantities. A gradual increase in bottle-making led to the adoption of a dark-green bottle glass by about 1630, in preference to the earlier product of lighter metal and colour. Several bottles and fragments in the London Guildhall Museum show the owner's seal and though this could not have been more than a sideline of the glass trade at the time, the bottle industry began to gain in importance about the period of the restoration. By 1677 several glasshouses concentrated on this particular branch of glass manufacture. One of the earliest intact examples is a bottle of the 'shaft and globe' design at the Northampton Museum, sealed and dated 1657, although earlier fragments may be seen in various national collections. Seals fused on to the bottle by pressing on a separate glass matrix are rarely of later date than 1680. Seals may take the form of plain initials or elaborately impressed medallions bearing crests and/or dates. After 1660 bottle necks began to diminish and by the end of the century the squat, onion-shaped wine bottle had become established. A general assumption is that the late-seventeenth-century product is somewhat broader at the shoulder than at the base, whereas in the early-eighteenth-century bottle the reverse applies. By the middle of the eighteenth century, body and neck had both grown taller, the shoulder had become less pronounced and the cylindrical bottle as we know it today had emerged (plate facing p. 80).

Pharmaceutical bottles of the late sixteenth and seventeenth centuries are frequent excavation finds. The colour of the metal varies from olive-green to blue or amber with often an attractive iridescence. Though sometimes reminiscent of Roman unguentaria or tear-bottles, the distinct neck and usually flat-rimmed orifice, together with a more or less pronounced kick in the base, leave little doubt as to correct identification of the seventeenth-century product (plate facing p. 17).

The outbreak of the Civil War caused an industrial eclipse which made itself felt in the glass trade, where Mansell's influence had begun to wane since the 1650s. The Company of Glaziers, who had been granted their first Charter by Charles I in 1635 as the Glass Seller's Company, was reconstituted in 1664. The Company soon showed itself as a sensible, if perhaps somewhat dictatorial, body of men who controlled the glass trade. As early as 1660 Mansell's monopoly had fallen into the hands of that enterprising meddler George Villiers, 2nd Duke of Buckingham (1627–88). He seems to have been a satisfactory front man for the Company, who were pleased to see his efforts in bringing the trade to the doors of the wealthy upper classes. His interests extended to experiments for production of a 'rock crystal' glass and he also began making mirrors at the Vauxhall plate glasshouse. The 'Royal Oak Goblet' (now in the U.S.A.) dated 1663, commemorating the marriage of Charles II with Catherine of Braganza, is ascribed to Buckingham's Greenwich glasshouse. It is a diamond-engraved goblet showing portraits of Charles and his queen and is light greenish with a mould-blown, knopped, Venetian stem. The glasses stemming from Buckingham's workshops are said to have been of good quality but of rather light, thinly blown metal. Several famous engraved 'flutes', such as the Exeter (Exeter Museum) and Scudamore (London Museum) flutes mentioned earlier, are attributed to the same glasshouse.

At the time of Mansell's patent, import of Venetian glass was prohibited to further the home industry but the demand for glassware had become so great that it was found necessary to lift the ban sometime after 1660. John Greene, one of the members of the Glass Sellers' Company, left explicit records of the type of glass imported from Murano. His first order to Alessio Morelli appears to have been placed in 1667 and descriptions are accompanied by precise sketches of the types of vessels suitable for the London market (Fig. 5). Most of these glasses seem somewhat delicate, confirmed by Greene's many complaints regarding the poor quality of the glass and the breakage caused in transit by inadequate packaging. The Company themselves felt the need for a more sturdy and serviceable glass

Fig. 5 Drawings based on John Greene's sketches accompanying
his Orders for Venetian Glass 1667–72

metal, and it is due to their initiative and perseverance that George Ravenscroft (1618–81) finally succeeded in developing his "crystalline glass resembling rock metal''—the flint glass or glass-of-lead. In Bohemia, as well as in Southern Germany, the fashion for wheel-engraving led to the development of a more robust glass metal, the potash lime glass. English lead crystal was the result of controlled experiments initiated by the Glass Sellers' Company, who were quick to recognize in Ravenscroft the ideal man for the job. A retired merchant and shipowner well acquainted with Venetian glass manufacture, Ravenscroft established his glasshouse in the Savoy in 1673. The following spring he was confident enough to apply for a patent to manufacture his new 'crystalline glass'. This was granted almost at once, in April 1674, and in 1676 the Company announced that a crystal glass had finally been perfected and any defects eliminated. In 1677 Ravenscroft endorsed this success by employing a seal, the Raven's Head, from the coat of arms of the Ravenscroft family, to mark his best specimens. Nevertheless, crizzling was not entirely eliminated until about 1685, when Ravenscroft's glasshouses at Henley and at the Savoy were in the hands of Hawley Bishopp and the manufacture of lead glass had become a matter of course. It must not be supposed, however, that all glass produced at this period was based on Ravenscroft's flint glass formula. Soda glass was made long after Ravenscroft's invention and was utilized for less important table-ware such a cruets and cheap tumblers. Furthermore, in common with Venetian cristallo, Ravenscroft's 'new flint glass' was at first blown rather thin and this resulted in the so-called 'single' flint, a fragile material and consequently extremely rare today. The improved 'double' flint or 'thick' flint glass was apparently made of a double gathering of the metal, and was developed in 1682. Ravenscroft retired in 1676 and died five years later. The glass made under his direction and that of Hawley Bishopp is a heavy metal with excellent refractive properties which fused at a lower temperature than the Venetian cristallo. The perfect specimens show a unique watery limpidity and clarity of colour but without the brittle hardness of surface, characteristic of the Venetian product (plate facing p. 49).

Ravenscroft period glass was made in a great variety of designs and types and this is shown even by the few surviving specimens bearing the

Raven's Head seal. Vertical ribbing and gadrooning, and twisted handles for larger pieces, were popular modes of decoration, and 'nipped diamond waies' are applied to several specimens. Posset pots, ewers, Roemers and flasks are among existing Ravenscroft pieces. Diamond engraving is extremely rare on glass of the Ravenscroft period and the most famous examples are probably the 'Buggin' bowls of crizzled lead glass. They were made on the occasion of the Wedding of Butler Buggin in 1676, and are engraved with the coats of arms of the couple. The bowls have now found separate homes; one may be seen at the Victoria and Albert Museum, the other in the Corning Museum of Glass, N.Y.

By the late seventeenth century a brief period of Baroque exuberance in English glass is represented by posset pots, bowls and large covered goblets adorned with a great variety of decoration. Prunts, gadrooning, nipped diamond waies and pincered decoration may all be found on the same specimen. Elaborate stems and finials shaped in the form of crowns, orbs and crosses are unmistakably English, whereas Netherlands and Venetian influence is noticeable in quatrefoil knops, certain adaptations of flügel glasses and attractive ale glasses and tumblers with writhen bowls.

During the last decade or so of the seventeenth century the English drinking glass emerged as an object with certain definable characteristics in form, substance and colour—the 'collector's period' had indeed begun. The baluster stem, the most important feature in the development of the drinking glass, was applied in a great number of variations. These have been arranged in the order of most likely appearance by W. A. Thorpe (*A History of English and Irish Glass*, London, 1929) as follows:

Inverted Baluster	1682–1710
Drop Knop	1690–1710
Angular Knop	1695–1715
Ball Knop	1695–1715
Multiple Knop	1700–1720
Annulated or Triple-ring Knop	1700–1725
Acorn Knop	1710–1715
Mushroom Knop	1710–1715
True Baluster	1710–1730

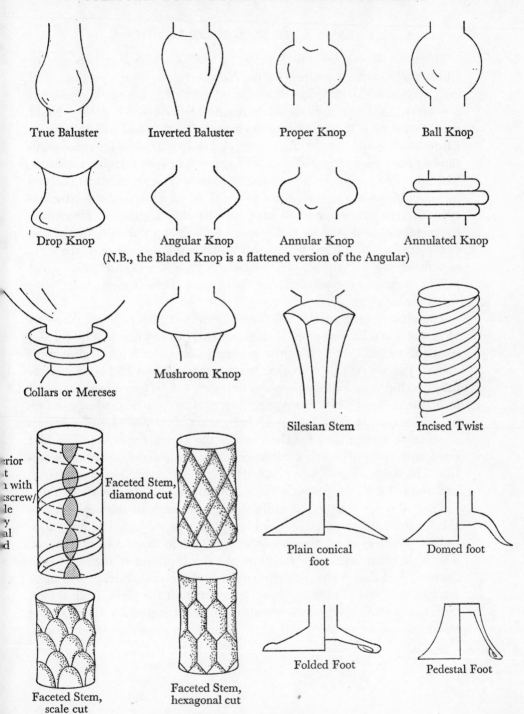

True Baluster Inverted Baluster Proper Knop Ball Knop

Drop Knop Angular Knop Annular Knop Annulated Knop

(N.B., the Bladed Knop is a flattened version of the Angular)

Collars or Mereses Mushroom Knop Silesian Stem Incised Twist

rior
t
with
screw/
le
y
al
d

Faceted Stem, diamond cut

Plain conical foot Domed foot

Faceted Stem, scale cut

Faceted Stem, hexagonal cut

Folded Foot Pedestal Foot

Fig. 6

From the Greene designs of glasses ordered from Venice, it is easy to follow through the transition to the baluster glass, which retains in its early stage a slight Venetian character. The new English metal, however, necessitated a design that would conform to the robust character of flint glass. Stems grow taller to form solid support for the bowl which becomes a little smaller and more straight-walled. The foot must be firm enough to support the glass and is folded under to form an edge of double thickness. The bowl often incorporates a thick solid base which sometimes encloses an air bubble, the origin of the tear which in turn inspired the later air-twist. Greene's restrained ball knop and baluster increase in dimension, the metal becomes heavier and assumes an 'oily' appearance. By the end of the century additional varieties of bowls begin to emerge in the form of waisted and bell shapes. The result is a glass of classic simplicity and perfect balance, expressing ideally the concept of the 'Queen Anne' style (plate facing p. 73).

The distinct greenish tint was common to lead glass between the years 1675 and 1700. Experiments to eliminate this tint resulted in a black, and sometimes bluish, hue, which is generally found in English glass until about 1730. By that time a colourless transparent glass had been success-fully developed and although colour tints may still be found in a weakened form, the brilliant white metal prevailing during 1730–80 made a wonderful foil for the sparkling colour- and air-twists of the period, providing an impeccable background for the work of the Dutch engravers. The best eighteenth-century glass is attributed to Newcastle and London manufacture. The Dagnia family, who founded their glasshouse in Newcastle in 1684, are credited with the perfection of a brilliant clear glass as early as 1725.

From the baluster period onward, right through to the beginning of the nineteenth century, the drinking glass was subjected to an extra-ordinary variety of manipulations with regard to shape and decoration. The folded foot becomes a rarity by the third quarter of the eighteenth century, and this is a logical consequence of the new, thicker and more serviceable metal. The most characteristic type is the plain, conical foot, i.e. a foot which rises toward the centre to meet the stem. A very flat foot should always be regarded with suspicion, even in glasses of earlier periods.

The terraced foot and the domed foot, folded, plain or moulded are variations greatly appreciated by the collector and are dependent upon the
whim and ability of the gaffer. They are frequently found on sweetmeats
and champagnes and achieve a harmonious balance between foot and
bowl design. By the late eighteenth century the square foot of Neo-classical
form had appeared and remained a feature with a variety of table-ware,
notably the 'rummer'. Several types of bowl had come into use by the
beginning of the eighteenth century and it is not safe to date a glass solely
on the basis of bowl design. Funnel and bell bowls, as well as flutes, were
accepted forms during the baluster period but the thistle and the double
ogee bowls, for instance, which were popular during the second and third
quarter of the eighteenth century, had already made rare appearances
before 1700. The most revealing part of the glass, however, is the stem,
and chronological classification of the eighteenth-century drinking glass is
based on the stem and its particular features. Published information is in
good agreement on the dating of stems, which may be grouped as follows:

Baluster Stems	1680–1730
Moulded Pedestal Stems (Silesian)	1714–65
Balustroid Stems	1725–60
Light (Newcastle) Balusters	1735–65
Airtwist stems	1730–70
Hollow Stems	1750–60
Incised Twist Stems	1750–65
Mixed and Colour Twist Stems	1755–75
Opaque White Twist Stems	1755–80
Faceted Stems	1760–1810

A plain, straight stem, and a composite stem made of plain and twist-
sections, occur during the years 1740–75, the latter group being something
of a rarity.

The 'Silesian' stem has no proven connection with Silesia, but is an
unusual stem form introduced from Germany and coinciding with the
accession of George I of Hanover in 1714. In its early form this moulded
pedestal stem is four-sided and sometimes impressed with the initial G.R.,
in honour of the king. In course of time the stem progressed to six- and

BOWL FORMS OF DRINKING GLASESS

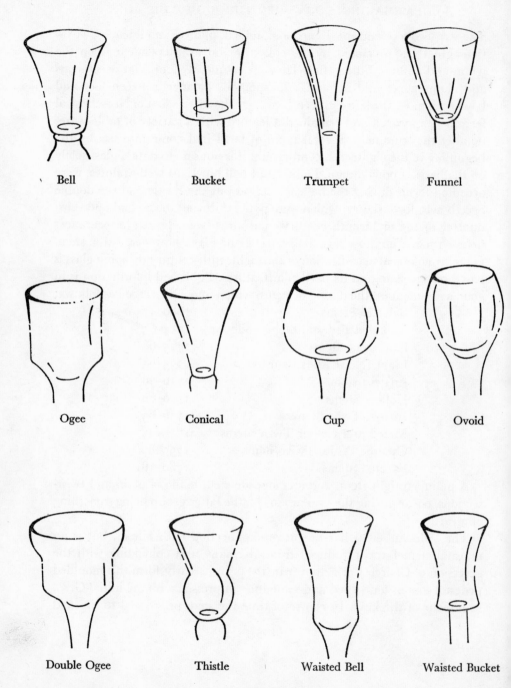

Bell	Bucket	Trumpet	Funnel
Ogee	Conical	Cup	Ovoid
Double Ogee	Thistle	Waisted Bell	Waisted Bucket

Fig. 7

eight-sided pedestals which became more and more elaborate and remained in favour until the mid-eighteenth century (plate facing p. 73). They were also applied to tableware such as candlesticks, sweetmeat glasses and tazza. Conical or domed, folded feet are a common feature of such stems but a cut and often scalloped foot may occur when this is in character with the design and decoration of the bowl, as, for instance, in sweetmeat glasses or champagnes.

The 'Balustroids' are regarded as the intermediary between the Baluster and the light (Newcastle) Baluster glass. Domed folded feet and trumpet, or waisted, bowls are frequently recurring features. The stems are usually tall and incorporate knops, swellings and balusters of less distinctive form, as is also the faint moulded decoration, sometimes aptly termed 'watermarking'. The metal is often of poor quality, especially in the later balustroid, and a certain amount of soda glass was also manufactured, mainly for export purposes. The slender 'Kitcat' glasses are attractive representatives of this group. The name is derived from an illustration of a gathering of the Kitcat club, with members using this type of drinking glass.

The Light Newcastle Baluster is one of the best and most elegant products of the English glasshouse. It is a tall glass which is often termed a goblet, and the brilliant white metal is of thinner and lighter quality than in the Baluster and Balustroid glasses. Bell and round funnel bowls, plain and waisted, occur most frequently, and their generous proportions provide added incentive for the engraver. The foot is usually not folded and a great variety of knopped stems, incorporating multiple tears and excellent interior twists, are a predominant feature of this Tyneside product (plate facing p. 73).

The earliest air-twist stems are represented in the drawn funnel, or drawn trumpet, a glass made in two sections, the bowl and stem and the welded-on foot. Stems are usually plain and incorporate single-series twists. With the manufacture of the three-section glass, where bowl, stem and foot are welded, manipulation is facilitated and twists are produced in a bewildering variety of patterns, some of which are shown (plate facing page 73.) Knopped twist stems, and rare triple series twists are much sought after by collectors and must be considered the gaffer's tour de force.

Wrythen glasses with or without stems are remnants of Venetian influence and remained popular throughout the eighteenth century. Both the wrythen or incised twist stem and the hollow stem were manufactured during a very short period and are consequently something of a rarity. Hollow stems are mostly cylindrical and separated from foot and bowl by knops or mereses. A twisted stem decoration could be achieved by rib-moulding and rib-twisting or by incising the still soft metal with an instrument and further twisting.

The variety and combination achieved in the manufacture of enamel twists is inexhaustible. Main types are the multiple spiral, the tape and the lace twists. Not long after the technique of the opaque white twist was perfected the colour variety came into fashion. All basic colours occur and may be combined with white, as well as air-twists. Particularly attractive are the gauze spirals edged in contrasting colours of blue, green and perhaps also red, achieving an alternating colour effect which is sometimes termed 'tartan'. A bright canary yellow is another rarity in this group of glasses, which are usually of very bright and fine quality metal. Stems are straight and feet are conical and fairly solid, and hardly ever folded. The preferred bowl form is ovoid.

A distinctive glass treatment is represented by the horizontal 'corrugate' rings characteristic of 'Lynn' glass. In 1693 a glasshouse in King's Lynn was owned by Francis Jackson and John Straw and there was another owned by Jonas Phillips in 1753. The warehouse of the Lynn factory was situated at Norwich and Lynn glass is therefore also referred to as Norwich glass. Various types of vessels made at Lynn show the characteristic rings. Opaque white twist stems occur frequently in 'Lynn wines, and a folded foot is not at all unusual.

The Glass Act of 1777–8 not only doubled the duty on lead glass but also imposed a tax on the actual enamel essential for making white or colour twists. The result was the almost immediate disappearance of this attractive and technically highly accomplished glass decoration.

The tall 'Toastmaster's' glass with its deceptive, thick-walled bowl holding only a few drops of liquid, and the 'Firing glass' with its unusually thick foot, made their appearance during the second quarter of the eighteenth century. Firing glasses were thumped on the table after a toast was given and this produced a sound not unlike a volley of guns. They are usually no higher than about 4 in. with short, thick stems, which may enclose enamel twists or be rudimentary only. Bowl forms are varied. The 'Hogarth' glass, recurring in paintings by this artist, is usually grouped with this family of glasses, but here the stem is missing entirely and the bowl set straight on to the foot with perhaps an interspaced knop or collar. The foot may be domed and folded, or it may be plain and thick as in the firing glass, usually about ¼ in. thick. Hogarth glasses were used for 'strong cordial water', because they are glasses of small capacity, but the term 'cordial glass' refers to a wineglass of normally proportioned foot and stem but relatively small bowl, holding at most 1½ oz. of liquid. A distinctive type of cordial is the 'Ratafia glass' with its long and narrow funnel bowl. Cordial glasses are also referred to as 'Drams'. Firing glasses are often associated with Freemasonry, and Masonic emblems may be found on the bowl.

The brilliancy of English metal is perhaps nowhere so elegantly ex-ploited as in cut decanters dating from the second half of the eighteenth century, although the earliest cut glasses are probably the scallop-edged, shallow-cut sweetmeat glasses of about 1720. The limitation in weight, imposed by the 1745 Glass Act, necessitated shallow cutting. Wineglasses of ovoid bowl shape with diamond and hexagonal cut stems appeared about this time and became more elaborate after 1760, when cut decora-tion extended to both foot and bowl. Fluted and scale cutting became fashionable and the wineglass incorporated a knopped stem (Fig. 6).

The rummer made its appearance about 1770. Although derived from the word 'Römer', this glass was used for the hot grog or toddy made with the addition of rum and it was a vessel of goblet size. The early rummer is distinguished by an ovoid-shaped bowl, a short cylindrical drawn stem and a circular foot. By the end of the century the bowl graduated to bucket shape, which was doubly annealed for heat resistance and rein-forced under the base by a welded-on disc. The square foot, which is usually moulded, appeared about 1800, by which time cut or engraved decoration may be found on the bowl.

After Admiral Rodney's victory over the Spanish Fleet in 1780 a special type of ship's decanter known as 'Rodney' became popular. It was of triangular silhouette, with a very broad base for stability and of special hardness due to additional annealing. The fashion for cutting ousted the plain 'Shaft and Globe' specimen and several designs of shouldered, barrel-shaped and tapering decanters evolved, tending towards a square or cylindrical shape by the early nineteenth century.

As early as 1718 a workshop was established by John Akerman & Son in London, where glass cutting was carried on quite successfully. A little later, about 1730, Thomas Betts opened his cutting shop where he employed both English and Continental workmen. The finest engraving, however, is generally attributed to the Dutch or Germans and for this purpose Newcastle glass was particularly suitable, as already mentioned. Commemorative glasses of all kinds became fashionable during the eighteenth century. Glasses recalling the two Jacobite rebellions of 1715 and 1745 constitute an important group of this type and they are usually divided into three sections. To the first belong glasses made prior to 1745. These are very rare and are engraved with the Stuart rose with leaves and buds, emblems of butterflies, stars, oakleaf, thistle. 'FIAT', the symbol of the Cycle Club, and the words 'Redeat' or 'Redi' are often added. The glasses themselves are of fine quality and proportion, since they were manufactured prior to the Excise Act. The second group consists of glasses decorated with more or less disguised pro-Jacobite symbols, such as the secret rose, which is formed by extending the cutting to the base of the bowl, so that when looking into it from above the pattern will show a design resembling a six-petalled rose. Flowers signified names; a Carnation stood for Charles Edward, Jasmine for James, and so on. The famous 'Amen' glasses with the concluding verse of the Jacobite Hymn most probably also belong to this second period, although some authorities suggest the earlier period. The third group was made after 1770, when the cause was hopelessly lost and there was no further need for caution or secrecy. Portrait glasses of the young Pretender are usually attributed to some date after 1745, and many of these fall into the third group of 1770 plus. Early Jacobite glasses may have very beautiful and elaborate stems incorporating air-twists, knops and enamel twists. Colour twist stems mostly belong to the third group. A charming series of commemorative glasses were made in Ireland, covering the rise of the House of Orange, and engraved glasses toasting the memory of William III were still made in 1830. 'Privateering' or nautical glasses are a further attraction for the collector, and coincide with the second and third phase of Jacobite glass. (Plate facing p. 73).

Oil gilding is found from about 1750 onward and the best period of enamelled decoration is attributable to the years 1760–80, when a colour-ful Rococo style had come to England from the Continent. Most of the artists we know by name were engaged in decorating both glass and porcelain, and it is no coincidence that some of the best enamelling is found on the opaque-white glass developed at Bristol soon after 1750. One of the finest Bristol enamellers was Michael Edkins (1733–1811). Opaque white vases, jars and beakers resembling Chinese porcelain in form and texture, and appropriately decorated with chinoiserie motifs in soft greens and reds with elegant birds and diaper border, are attributed to this artist. He may also have been responsible for the charming enamelled tea canisters decorated with colourful birds and foliage. In London, enamel-ling and gilding of beakers, scent bottles, cruets, toilet bottles and decanters was done by a most prolific and able artist, James Giles (1713–80). Giles's work is a direct result of the Adams style and motifs vary from chinoiserie to elegant classical designs of urns, flowers and birds (pheasants). His work is found on opaque white as well as coloured glass and his medium was almost exclusively confined to gilding. Cut coloured glass scent bottles decorated in this manner are typical examples of Giles's work. During the years 1775 to at least 1805 the Jacobs family were making and gilding Bristol blue glass at their Non-such Flint Glass Manufactory. Their work is usually signed and a favourite decorative motif, the Empire-inspired frieze of key fret pattern, occurs frequently. They are thought to have also employed Edkins. (Plate facing p. 112.)

A branch of the Dagnia family founded the earliest recorded glasshouse at Bristol in 1651. White opaque and blue transparent glass is generally attributed to Bristol manufacture but this was also produced in other areas, particularly in the Midlands. What may be true is that greater quantities of opaque white and blue glass were manufactured at Bristol than elsewhere and that the white was whiter, the blue a finer and deeper blue and the quality superior in the local product. (Plate facing p. 97).

The most gifted and original of the glass enamellers were William Beilby Jr. (1740–1819) and his sister Mary (1749–97), who worked together until about 1778. The Beilbys were employed at the Newcastle glasshouse of Dagnia-Williams, where they had at their disposal some of the finest glass in England. They were exceptionally versatile artists and their work is associated with both monochrome white and coloured enamelling. A very faint white enamelling is rather rare and must date from an early experimental stage. Most Beilby glasses have opaque white twist stems and some of the coloured enamelling of heraldic type is found on large bucket bowl goblets with enamel twist stems. Air-twists and more rarely, incised-twist glasses are also found decorated by the Beilbys. The fruiting vine was a favourite subject and this is often executed in monochrome white with a faint bluish tinge. Nowhere is Rococo influence stronger than in the work of this industrious pair, expressed in rural scenes of hunting and boating, in the scroll work and wreaths of flowers and in the delightful charm with which the motifs are illustrated. Between 1762 and 1778 the Beilbys did some portrait work, mostly of Jacobite interest. Brother and sister signed their work on occasion but only with the family name. The rose is attributed to the hand of Mary. (Plate facing p. 81.)

In 1777, the glass tax was doubled and two years later Ireland was granted full freedom of trade. English glassmakers quickly saw the advantage of moving to tax-free Ireland and from 1780 to 1825 we may speak of an Anglo-Irish period. In 1783 John Hill, of Stourbridge, was financed by the Penrose brothers to establish the Waterford glass factory. The 'blue' tint of Waterford glass has proved somewhat mythical and applies generally to unsuccessfully decolourized glass. A triple ring and mushroom stopper is associated with Waterford decanters and a mark 'Penrose Waterford' may be found below the base until just after 1800. Typical cutting is of broad bands, squares or scalloped pendants filled out with a

'Non-Such' Bristol blue wineglass cooler with gilt Greek key pattern border at the rim, and swags of flowers and leaves beneath the lips. Signed 'I. Jacobs, Bristol', c. 1805. Ht. 10 cm.

'Nailsea' type jug of the early 19th century. Dark-green glass with opaque white flecks marvered in and an opaque-white thread round the rim. Ht. 24 cm.

Cut-glass snuffbottle with sulphide portrait, perhaps representing Alexander the Great. Attributed to Apsley Pellatt, but possibly French, c. 1820–1825. Ht. 7 cm.

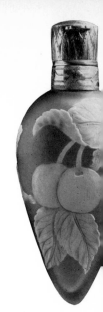

Scent bottle in cameo glass with opaque white cherries and leaves on a pale blue ground and a silver screw top, probably made by Thomas Webb & Sons, Stourbridge, in 1887. Length: about 10 cm.

Victorian scent- and smelling-bottles, the majority double-ended in coloured, cut and faceted glass. Ht. 7·5–12·5 cm.

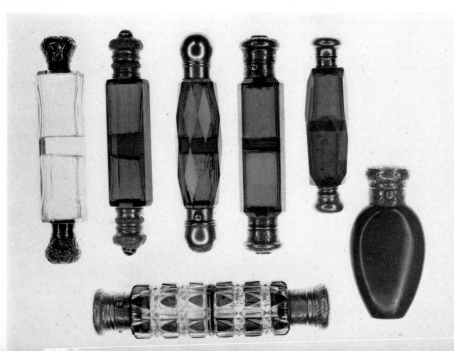

fine criss-cross pattern. The Cork Glass Company, founded at the same time and closing down in 1818, was more enterprising in design than Waterford and a favourite cutting device was produced by the vesica pattern. A moulded factory mark may appear on the base. The Waterloo Company was in existence from 1815–35 only; occasionally a firm's mark is found but looped or knotted rope engraving is frequently identified with this glasshouse. The mark 'Edwards Belfast' refers to a factory founded by a Bristol glassmaker about 1781. Two triangular neck-rings and a tapering-shape decanter, of Bristol design, is typical of this Belfast firm. In Dublin, Charles Mulvany established his glasshouse in 1785, with the maker's mark 'C.M. & Co.', but other marks such as 'Francis Collins Dublin' and 'Mary Carter & Son' are thought to refer to traders and not to actual manufacturers.

Due to the unrestricted use of lead, glass of the earlier Anglo-Irish period may be distinguished by thicker metal, deeper cutting and a certain heaviness of form in comparison with the English product. Feet are often moulded. During 1800–10 Irish cutting was at its best, incorporating additional styles such as reeding, cross-cut diamond, strawberry diamond, hobnail and, most elegant of all, horizontal prismatic. A revival of the classical taste as advocated by the Adam brothers are slim, oval forms of distinctive simplicity. This period also saw the rise in popularity of the chandelier, which became increasingly endowed with all the refinements of the cutter's craft. The flat glass drops with scalloped, bevelled edges associated with early-eighteenth-century chandeliers, gave way to elaborate diamond and prismatic cutting. A refined luxury for the superbly set-out table were matching pairs of table chandeliers or sconces, with glittering drops and festoons. The gaining popularity of Wedgwood's Jasper ware often resulted in a pleasing combination of Wedgwood and crystal, in the typical elegant Adam style. Forms become heavier during the Regency period and cutting more elaborate. During the mid-Victorian era turn-over bowls, boat-shaped dishes and celery vases retain the character of earlier periods but the metal may affect an unpleasant, yellowish tone, and cutting tends to be over-elaborate.

In 1788 three brothers-in-law, John Robert Lucas, William Chance and

Edward Homer, founded a glasshouse at Nailsea, which soon attracted workers from nearby Bristol. The then existing tax on bottle-glass was but a fraction of that imposed on flint glass. Cullet from Bristol 'white' glasshouses was relatively cheap and easy to obtain and the characteristic dark green Nailsea glass with fused-on enamel chips of varying colour was the result of an ingenious exploitation of bottle-glass (plate facing p. 112). An attractive effect was achieved by applying bands of enamel to a soft green, transparent metal. The glassware decorated in this manner has a 'country market' style which is functional as well as pleasing. More sophisticated products ascribed to Nailsea, but certainly also made elsewhere (Bristol, Stourbridge) around the 1830s, are the clear or lightly tinted transparent gimmel flasks, bellow flasks, jars with covers and a variety of other more fanciful objects with attractive combed or latticinio effects. The 'Nailsea rolling-pin' with inscribed motto and splashed, banded or varied decoration, was a souvenir manufactured in many coastal towns.

The original Nailsea works closed in 1869 but the Nailsea style was copied in Birmingham, Warrington and many of the northern glassmaking centres well into the late Victorian era. The Scottish bottle-making industry at Alloa attracted several Nailsea glassworkers and as a result a typical 'Nailsea' decorative effect was achieved with loops and bands in opaque enamel. The existing link between Scottish and English glasshouses was initiated during the Mansell period. During the mid-nineteenth century, engraving received a new impetus due to emigrant Bohemian workmen but the chief influence came from Stourbridge men who established themselves in the main Scottish glassmaking areas around Edinburgh and Glasgow. An original note was introduced in the late nineteenth century by the Glasgow firm of James Couper & Sons with a bubbly and streaky glass metal called 'Clutha' glass. The effect is distinctly 'Art Nouveau' and a similar idea is expressed in the 'Monart' ware of the 1920s, a splashed and streaky coloured product of heavy metal and solid form, made by Moncrieff's Glass-Works at Perth, and probably influenced by a Spaniard, Salvador Ysart, who came to Moncrieff's in 1922.

Apsley Pellatt (1791–1863) and his process of cristallo-ceramie has been mentioned earlier. Pellatt was greatly influenced by James Tassie (1735–

1799) and his nephew William (1777–1860), who revived a fashion for cameo cutting with their glass paste portraits and medallions in opaque white relief. The repeal, in 1845, of the Glass Excise Act produced a feverish activity in the glass industry. The Great Exhibition of 1851 was proof that Bohemian techniques of cutting, casing and colouring glass were applied in English factories, though crudely at first. As in France, the glass industry profited by the emergence of individual glass artists, with particular emphasis on the Stourbridge area. During the 1870s William Fritsche, a landlord at Dennis, produced some remarkable engraving in the best tradition of Bohemian rock crystal style, and a versatile Bohemian artist, Frederick Kny, created some fine crystal engraving which was equalled by John Northwood I (1836–1902). The Elgin marbles were a favourite subject with artists of this period, during which a remnant of the classical style was still kept alive. The most dynamic name in the Stourbridge industry is that of Thomas Webb, first upon the scene as Webb & Richardson in 1833. There was constant movement in the ownership of Stourbridge glasshouses, affiliations were formed and broken up and the same firm might be subjected to a consecutive change of name, with the best artists working for several factories. Henry G. Richardson & Sons and Thomas Webb & Company are both still at Dennis today. In 1876 John Northwood completed his replica of the Portland Vase and thus created the most important piece of English cameo glass. The Northwood school of cameo technique had its academic roots in the Government School of Design, founded in Stourbridge in 1852. John Northwood II, the son, and the nephews, continued in the tradition of classical subjects but the famous Woodall brothers, George (1850–1925) and Tom, nephews of the gifted enameller Thomas Bott, went beyond the limitations of classical motifs with stylized flowers and fruit and all-over formal patterns of sometimes Italianate, sometimes oriental character. The white raised motif on pink-brownish ground is the usual colouring associated with cameo glass but a variety of shades are found, ranging from a delicate yellow to a midnight blue as basic colour tone. Thomas Webb's companies employed and financed most of the best cameo artists at one time or other, and in consequence English glass made by this technique is referred to as 'Webb's

Cameo Glass' even if no signature is present. The Woodall team consisted of about seventy craftsmen and obviously many of the artists produced work in similar style. It was a perfectionist art where artists designed their own tools as Gallé had done and the ultimate achievement was of the highest artistic and technical merit. Acid etching was also applied in cameo cutting techniques. (Plate facing p. 113.)

By 1830 the American pressed-glass technique had reached England and by the middle and late nineteenth century several novelty-type wares appeared on the market. Much of this pressed glass was of opaque, streaky metal termed 'slag glass', since it was produced by deliberately introducing slag, i.e., waste-material obtained from metal foundries. The prettiest slag glass is of a bright, translucent blue, well matched by the 'Biedermeier' period blue glass of Bohemian, Austrian or German manufacture, though other colours such as purple, cream and black are found. The patterns of jugs, plates, dishes, candlesticks and other ware remained fairly repetitive throughout their period of popularity from *c.* 1875 to 1890. Slag glass often bears a maker's mark and a registration mark indicating date. Firms associated with this glassware are Sowerby & Co. of Gateshead, mark: peacock's head (plate facing p. 88). Greener & Co. of Sunderland, mark: lion facing left, bearing halberd; George Davidson & Co. of Gateshead, mark: lion on rampart, facing right. Webb's brought out their famous 'Queen's Burmese', a semi-opaque glass shaded from salmon pink to yellow, originally patented in 1885 by the American Mount Washington Glass Co., New Bedford, Mass. A variety of night-lights, dishes and vases were made and the Webb product was usually signed. Iridescent glass was also made at this late period particularly by Powell's of Whitefriars Glass Works, but French-inspired paper-weights were produced at Birmingham and Stourbridge from the middle of the century onward. Stourbridge specialities are weighted ink bottles and tumblers, and the work seems perfectly good, though less imaginative than the French product. The process of colour lithography was perfected during the 1850s and transfer printing by this method became an additional glass decoration at that time.

Many of the old glassmaking firms have survived and flourish today.

On the industrial side we have Chance Bros. and Pilkingtons, and Brierley (Hill), Webb and Whitefriars are some of the firms that produce fine-quality cut crystal, incorporating many new artistic trends.

America

Glassmaking was first introduced in America by English settlers who had arrived in Jamestown in 1608. Early American glass was of coarse, bubbly greenish texture, which developed later to a blue or brownish tinted metal. The Jamestown attempts, as well as several others, were soon abandoned and there was no successful glass manufacture until 1739, when Caspar Wistar established his factory in Salem County, Southern New Jersey. Brown, amber, green, blue and turquoise vessels with spirally wound threads near the top and a wave pattern around the base are characteristic of Wistarberg glass. A factory at Kensington, Pennsylvania, later known as the Dyottville Glass Works, had been in operation since 1771 but the factory at Glassboro, New Jersey, became the real successor to Wistarberg when the original glasshouse ceased manufacture in 1780, and the workmen joined nearby Glassboro. Under the Wistarberg influence a free-blown glass style of good line and attrative shape developed, known as the South Jersey style. South Jersey glass was made in a variety of colours, predominantly amber, green and aquamarine, and a typical decorative theme often present is the lily-pad motif, vaguely resembling a lily pad and perhaps developed originally from European flammiform gadrooning. By the early nineteenth century additional effects were achieved by application of looped or swirled opaque colour bands and trailed, pinched or crimped decoration.

In 1763 a colourful and extravagant personality, Henry William Stiegel, appeared on the American glassmaking scene. Stiegel attempted glass-making in the German manner and during 1763 and 1774 he produced pieces of good quality and sophisticated design, which were often indistinguishable from Continental glass. Workmen from many Continental countries were employed at the glasshouses of Elizabeth Furnace and at Manheim, Pennsylvania. The most distinctive Stiegel glass is of rich blue or amethyst colour, with expanded mould-blown pattern and a clear, resonant ring. Enamelling of the German, rustic type, and wheel engraving occur frequently and are ably done, and a mould-blown pattern incorporating the 'daisy in a diamond' design is particularly associated with Stiegel ware.

Another German glass manufacturer, John Frederick Amelung, established an even more ambitious industry in 1784. Amelung's glasshouse near Frederick, Maryland, was named the New Bremen Glass Manufactory after his home town. Amelung's glass shows expert craftsmanship, and both metal and design were of high standard. Covered goblets and presentation glasses (plate facing p. 145) were a speciality and the engraving of heraldic motifs and Rococo scrollwork was carried out in the best German manner by German craftsmen. Unfortunately, the glasshouse could not hold its own for more than a brief decade and the Amelung glassworkers were absorbed by other factories. One of these was started by a Swiss, Albert Gallatin, in 1797. Aptly named the New Geneva Glassworks, this factory was situated in western Pennsylvania and produced glass of plain shape and predominantly pale green or yellow. Manufacture ceased in 1807 but by then several glasshouses in New York State were producing glass in the South Jersey style in which the lily-pad motif was frequently employed. Some of the most attractive colours applied are clear aquamarines or light greens (plate facing p. 160).

The perfection of a practical glass-pressing machine, with which molten glass could be pressed into any desired shape in a hand-operated mould, revolutionized American and European glass industries. The rapid new process, patented in 1827, was eminently suitable to meet the demands of a mass market and a further advantage was gained by the use of a three-part, hinged mould. The collector might note that early American pressed glass was not hand-finished and rough edges may remain at mould seams. Between 1827 and 1850 several factories, in particular the New England Glass Company (1818–88) and the Boston and Sandwich Glass Company (1825–88), produced glass of a distinctive, similar design. This was the so-called 'Lacy', achieved by small dots in the mould producing a stippled appearance designed to give an overall lacy effect, which left no part of the surface untouched (plate facing p. 161).

Free-blown glass in green and amber was produced during the late eighteenth and early nineteenth centuries by several of the local glass companies and by 1840 attractive colours of peacock blue, purple, opaque white and yellow were applied. The charming violin bottles (see Terminology) belong to this period. Well-designed shapes tended toward the late Empire and Regency style which lent itself admirably to opaque glass. Subtle effects were achieved in opalescent glass and during the late nineteenth century a small number of objects were made in the 'vitro-di-trina' technique at the Sandwich factory. At the same time there was a revival in the art of cutting due to Irish and English influence, with a decisive leaning toward Continental glass styles, particularly at the New England factory. A fascinating section of glassmaking is represented by paperweights produced during the period 1850–80 by the New England and the Boston & Sandwich glass companies in particular. Apart from millefiori weights and skilfully produced, pressed and acid-treated portraits set in a faceted, clear glass matrix, much originality is shown in the weights of coloured, almost life-size glass fruit resting on a clear glass cushion.

The year 1878 saw the formation of Louis C. Tiffany Company, Associated Artists, and in 1880 its founder patented an iridescent glass technique by the name of 'Favrile'. Louis Comfort Tiffany (1848–1933), son of New York's most fashionable jeweller, Charles Tiffany, whose establishments and connections were world-wide, studied painting in New York and Paris and often visited his father's shop in London's Regent Street. As so many artists of the *art nouveau* period, he developed a taste for the oriental and many of his most lavish interior-decorating schemes reflect this mood. His work in this field, which included re-decoration of parts of the White House, combined all the lavish vulgarity of the American millionaire with expert craftsmanship and controlled taste. His interest in glass as a decorative material began with experiments in stained windows as early as 1872. To the young Tiffany it was the glass metal itself that seemed the dominant material to which the figurative should be subjected. He exploited more fully than perhaps any other of his contemporaries the fusible properties of glass in all its subtle nuances. Favrile was a deliberate attempt to imitate the iridescence of antique glass. Astonishing colour schemes such as a brilliant peacock blue, or a warm golden glow, were achieved in this technique, by which the hot glass object was subjected to metallic vapours, which in turn were absorbed by the glass surface to form layers of scintillating rainbow colour. By allowing the coloured glass mass to flow freely, Tiffany created abstract patterns which were often reflected in the delicate shape of the object itself, as for instance in the peacock vases. Most Favrile was thin blown and consequently light in weight, but in response to Gallé's work cameo glass was made for a brief period. Pieces of heavier glass with pitted surfaces or covered with thick metallic films were also made in Tiffany's workshop, and Pazaurek in his *Moderne Gläser* (Leipzig, 1901) speculates whether these objects have a legitimate right to be classed as glass. The name 'Tiffany Glass and Decorating Company' was adopted in 1892 and in 1900 Tiffany Studios employed hundreds of workers, many of them women, under Tiffany's careful supervision. The 1900 Paris Exhibition proved that iridescent glass was a great success and several manufacturers followed in Tiffany's footsteps, although a Hungarian-developed, iridescent glass had already been shown at the 1873 Vienna World Exhibition and Webb experimented in iridescence as early as 1878. The glass made at the Bohemian factory of Joh. Lötz Witwe in Klostermühle is probably one of the best products of this Tiffany-inspired phase and the *Papillon Glas* with its butterfly-wing effect—a costly process—is typical of Lötz at its best. Josef Pallme König of Steinschönau und Kosten, Graf Harrach at Neuwelt, and J. & L. Lobmeyr of Vienna are some of the more important factories that produced iridescent glass of artistic quality.

Tiffany glass is usually signed under the base. The signature may consist of the initials L.C.T. only, or it may be in full, when it is often preceded by certain numerals. The word 'Favrile' may be added to the signature or it may be found on a separate stuck-on label (plate facing p. 145).

The artistic treatment of luxury ware produced by the Steuben Glass Company once again elevates glass to the realm of precious materials, with which it is often embellished. The factory grew from the Corning Glass Works which were established by an Englishman, Frederick Carder,

Russian tea caddies, 1870–80: *left to right*, moulded caddy in turquoise opaline glass, decorated with Chinese-style figures and inscriptions in Chinese and Russian. Ht. 16 cm.; moulded caddy, transparent colourless glass, ruby-flashed, impressed on base Russian Imperial Eagle and the name of the factory, "Mal'tzov". Ht. 9·5 cm.; moulded caddy, transparent, deep-blue glass, also from the Mal'tzov factory and impressed on base with Russian Imperial Eagle. Ht. 11 cm.

in 1903. In 1933 a grandson, Arthur Amory Houghton Jr., took over the Steuben Division of the works and founded a company which aimed at "highest standards of design, quality and workmanship". A crystal glass of exceptional quality was the result, fine enough to encourage many of the world's leading contemporary artists, such as Laurence Whistler, to make some unique and exquisitely engraved pieces, several of which have become cherished museum exhibits.

France

The oldest glass found in France dates from the time of Roman occupation, when the craft was introduced. Cups and vessels from Franco-Merovingian burial places do not differ greatly from the greenish or yellowish glass objects with prunts or trails found in Britain and elsewhere. The stained glass in the district of Poitou clearly shows that glazier settlements were in existence in France during the twelfth century, if not earlier. The feudal system, under which the nobility was in possession of large and wooded territories, encouraged glassmaking much in the same way as its Bohemian counterpart. The landowners established glasshouses in the hope of creating a profitable business but the fortunes and, more often, misfortunes were borne by the workers themselves. Many of the craftsmen had originally arrived from Italian glassmaking centres and it was usual for several families to settle on one estate, to intermarry and produce future generations of glassmakers. Glasshouses were in production in Provence and Normandy as early as the thirteenth century and the system of small family firms of glasshouses scattered over many wooded areas persisted until the end of the eighteenth century, often existing under great hardship. In 1466 glassworkers at La Ferrière in Poitou presented twelve dozen glasses and one dozen ewers to the Abbess of the Holy Cross, at Poitiers, in exchange for permission to collect fern for use as fuel. In 1572 Fabriano Salviati from Murano began making glass *à la façon de Venise* in Poitou and in 1490 glassmakers in France obtained the right to style themselves *'gentilhommes verriers'*. This title applied equally to the impoverished nobility turned glassmaker perforce. A good number of Huguenot noblemen devoted their efforts to this industry since it was a trade that would not disgrace rank. There is record that in 1746 forty *gentilhommes verriers* from Gascony were sent to the gallows for professing the principles of the reformation. In 1558 Henry II brought two Mantua glassmakers to Rouen to make glass *à la façon de Venise* and in 1603 Henry IV established the glassworks at Paris and Nevers. In 1664 the minister of Louis XIV begged the Bishop of Béziers, French ambassador to Venice, to send some glassworkers to France. The ambassador replied that if he did so he might be thrown into the sea. Nevertheless, a year later eighteen Venetians were bribed sufficiently to come to work in Paris and the foundation was laid for a French mirror industry. At the same time Richard Lucas was making mirrors at Tours-la-Ville near Cherbourg and the intelligent chief minister united the two glassworks and prohibited import of mirrors from Venice. The established method of mirror manufacture was by applying metal foil to glass obtained by the broadsheet technique. The necessary flattening of the glass cylinder caused a variety of blemishes on the surface, with the final result of frequent distortions. In 1688 a process of casting large plateglass was perfected and the factory which was eventually established by Louis Lucas de Nehou in 1695 at St. Gobain is today one of the largest in the world. The French monopoly for plate-glass manufacture lasted for over a hundred years until England established a plate-glass works in 1773 at Ravenhead, Lancs. The casting hall, which had a length of 113 yd. and a width of 50 yd., still exists in part and now belongs to Pilkingtons, who have made their own revolutionary contribution to sheet manufacture by their float glass process. In 1699 mirrors were still rare and costly and the Countess of Fiesque declared that she had done "something very clever indeed" when she sold part of her land, which only brought in corn, and bought herself a magnificent mirror with the proceeds.

Attractive enamelling is found on some of the rare sixteenth-century goblets and chalices still in existence. This type of decoration was mostly done to order and the high cost would account for its rarity. A chalice in the Wallace Collection shows the influence of the *façon de Venise* but the enamelling and style of design is less 'fussy' than the Venetian counterpart. The actual decoration might have been carried out by Venetian craftsmen but the two marriage goblets (one in the British Museum, the other in the Toledo Museum, U.S.A.) show a similar, uncluttered simplicity of enamelled design, and this fact points to a definite style evolved in a French workshop (plate facing p. 65).

Quite different was the work of the so-called 'glass enamellers' at the end of the sixteenth and during the early seventeenth centuries. These are the small 'grotesques' made at the lamp in a variety of miniature models representing comedy figures or subjects of classical or religious character. Tableaux of astonishing complexity and small grottos like shrines were assembled, usually by nuns. In 1605 reference was made to "little dogs of glass and other animals made at Nevers" as favourite toys of the little Louis (XIII). Nevers, some sixty miles from Paris, records a fair number of glassblowing families in its parish register. *Verre filé de Nevers* was made for at least three centuries and manufacture was not solely confined to Nevers. The glass threads from which Nevers figurines are made are all wired with copper, unless the glass is too fine. Animal shapes are hollow blown and very thin glass threads, *verre frisé*, form the applied decorative effects. Single figures had stands made of trailed *verre filé*; where a stand is missing, the figure is usually broken off from an ensemble. Barrington Haynes feels that *verre filé de Nevers* suggests a childlike mind but the assumption by H. Clouzot in his article on the subject (*La Rennaissance*, 1924) of a local art often practised by innkeepers, explains much of the native charm of these gay little glass objects. On a distinctly higher artistic level was the work produced in the Orleans glasshouse of Bernard Perrot, or Perrotto as he is referred to by Hartshorne. Perrot, an able and enterprising glassmaker, inherited the monopoly of supplying glass throughout the area along the River Loire. He was active during the last thirty or forty years of the seventeenth century. Hartshorne quotes a source which states that Perrot had invented a process for casting glass "de faire couler le cristal en table comme des metaux" as early as 1662, and that already before 1666 he made use of anthracite as fuel. He produced mould-blown glass vessels of originality and charm, with fleurs-de-lys and hearts motifs recurring frequently (pl. facing p. 65). A Venetian influence is often apparent, and he is also credited with having re-developed marbled and opaque coloured glass. At this time, no distinctive national style had developed in French drinking glasses, and large quantities of diverse glass-ware were imported from neighbouring countries. The candlesticks, ewers, light wineglasses and small cordials produced in French glasshouses are often difficult to distinguish from glass made elsewhere, and styles were borrowed from the Netherlands, England and Bohemia. The foundations of a French glass industry were laid in October 1764, when the Bishop of Metz, Mgr. de Montmorency-Laval, obtained permission from Louis XV to establish the glasshouse of Sainte-Anne, at Baccarat, and began the manufacture of table- and window-glass. After a series of misfortunes, commencing with the depression prior to the French Revolution, the factory was purchased for 862 hectogrammes of fine gold by Monsieur d'Artigues, owner of a glassworks at Vonêche in Belgium. Between 1817 and 1822 the firm traded under the name 'Vonêche Baccarat' and con-centrated on the manufacture of lead crystal. In 1822 the factory changed hands again and the 'Compagnie des Cristalleries de Baccarat' was established. Opaline and agate glass was manufactured at Baccarat from 1823 and during the following twenty years a variety of coloured crystal glass was developed, including the 'cristal dichroide', a glass of strong green or yellow colouring similar to Riedel's *Annagrün* and *Annagelb*, and obtained by the same technique.

One of the most influential personalities in French glassmaking history was George Bontemps, employed at the glassworks of Choisy-le-Roi in Paris from 1823 to 1848. His experiments with Bohemian and Venetian techniques, and the re-creation of latticinio and millefiori glass, encouraged contemporary French factories to embark on similar paths. The result was that colourful extravaganza the French paperweight. (Pl. facing p. 97.)

Names mainly associated with the manufacture of paperweights are Baccarat, St. Louis and Clichy. The earliest Baccarat millefiori weights were put on the market in 1846 and, if dated, they will be from 1846–9 inclusive, the last year being also the rarest. Dates are preceded by the letter 'B' and initials without date probably represent the workman's signature. The manufacture of Baccarat 'sulfures', enclosing flowers, bouquets, fruit or animals, began in 1848 and was soon followed by paper-weights decorated with cristallo-ceramie, the so-called 'sulphides'. By this technique ornaments, and in particular medallions, of metallic or refractory nature, were enclosed in a clear glass matrix which was often further embellished by facet-cutting. 'Sulfures' and 'sulphides' were manufactured until the beginning of this century and cut and faceted beakers with cristallo-ceramie and added colourful (tricolor) enamelling were a Baccarat speciality. St. Louis specimens were dated during the years 1847–9, with the initials 'SL' preceding. Specimens have been found marked with later dates but this is rare and, as in the case of certain Baccarat weights dated after the year 1850, they were made for presentation purposes. The St. Louis factory was perhaps a little more imaginative in design and the best snake weights were made at this glasshouse. Snake and similar reptile weights are much sought after and a great number of them appeared at the Farouk sale in 1954. A flattened dome seems characteristic for some paperweights of St. Louis manufacture. The design of Clichy weights is more conventional, although the Clichy swirl pattern is quite distinctive. A full signature is rare but the initial 'C' seems to be more usual. It must be remembered that only a relatively small number of weights bear signatures and these are usually incorporated in the pattern, toward the side. Overlay weights in a variety of attractive colours, with windows cut to reveal the pattern inside, are a greatly cherished collector's item and were produced by all three factories. The overlay often has an opaque white lining which shows to advantage with facet cutting, and this decoration is usually termed 'double' overlay and occasionally incorporates gilding. Miniature weights of $1\frac{1}{2}$ to 2 in. diameter and magnum weights of 1 in. larger than the average size of about 3 in. across were also made by the three companies. Baccarat magnums may often be distinguished by a star-cut base. Paperweights are priced according to the rarity of their colour and design; a unique yellow overlay weight of St. Louis manufacture was sold in 1957 for £2,700 and in 1969 rare weights have fetched £5,000 and more. Millefiori canes showing figured silhouettes appear in weights made by Baccarat and St. Louis. Detailed information on the characteristic features and classification of paperweights will be found in *Les Presses Papiers*, by R. Imbert and Y. Amic, Paris, 1948; *Paperweights and other Glass Curiosities*, by E. M. Elville, London,

1954; and *Antique French Paperweights*, by P. Jokelson, New York, 1955.

In 1867 Baccarat began engraving by the wheel and at the Paris Exhibition of 1878 highly accomplished decoration of this type accentuated the brilliance and purity of Baccarat crystal. The over-ornate glitter resulting from the popularity of new pressing techniques which facilitated mass production was not to remain unchallenged. From small French studio workshops emerged a highly individualistic form of glass art which combined ancient modes of decorative processes with a naturalistic style. At the centre of this 'naturalist' movement associated with *art nouveau* stood the Ecole de Nancy with Emile Gallé (1846–1904) as its inspiring force. Gallé's father, Charles, was a successful designer of luxury faience and furniture. His mother added a mirror factory to the family fortune, and this was supplemented by the production of table-glass. Emile was a poet born into the trade and although he designed both ceramics and furniture it was in the subtlety of the glass material that he could best express the sensitive lyricism of his artistic inspirations. That he was successful beyond his most ambitious dreams was due to a life-time of passionate research and unceasing labour. The driving force in Gallé's creative work was nature herself in all her moods and nuances and his first aims were to express naturalistic forms in his chosen material. During the earliest period Gallé concentrated on decorative embellishment rather than on manipulation and transformation of the actual metal. His primary decorative technique consisted of enamelling and the first specimens produced soon after the establishment of the factory in Nancy in 1874 appear somewhat crude. They are signed, as are indeed all pieces from Gallé's workshops, usually in brown enamel or gilt, with the artist's own signature in a neat, controlled hand. By 1878 Gallé's creative style had undergone a great change and his finest work was produced from this period onward. He had learned to obtain from the potmetal whatever his artistic inspiration demanded and whether his material is of limpid transparency or of translucent colour, whether the treatment is figurative or abstract, the decorative effect achieved by cutting or engraving, enamelling or fusion of varicoloured glass masses, every piece is created as an expression of the artist's highest ideals. Gallé's concept of nature seen through the eyes of poetry and lyricism is represented by the unique work produced during the last fifteen years of the nineteenth century, when the poetic feeling with which he imbued his substance did not seem expressive enough. Inspiration came from verses or fragments of romantic symbolism which were inscribed upon the glass, and the *verreries parlantes* and *vases de tristesses* are representative of these emotions. Signatures are of infinite variety and may be found engraved or enamelled on the base within the design of a tree, a flower, a mushroom, emphasizing again the artist's affinity with nature. The Croix de Lorraine emblem may also be incorporated. Gallé took his inspiration from East and West, and the effects achieved by eighteenth-century Chinese and Japanese artists in the techniques of overlay glass inspired him in a revival of a cameo glass art, by fusing and subsequent carving of at first clear and coloured, later opaque-coloured glass masses. Cameo glass of the so-called opaque period between 1884 and Gallé's death in 1904 shows engraved or carved signatures on the plainest part of the surface. In many cases the signature agrees with and almost becomes part of the decorative character. By that time the Gallé factory had become a successful commercial venture and due to increased production similar motifs, forms and colours occur frequently. Vases and lamps decorated with flowers and plants of pale mauve, purple or greenish tone on frosted ground are typical of this late period. Decorative treatment was speeded up by eventual introduction of acid etching, a process not favoured by Gallé himself, who had designed his own cutting tools. After Gallé's death and until 1914 the factory continued under the guidance of Gallé's friend, the painter Victor Prouvé, and glass made during this period bears the Gallé signature preceded by a small star. Work recommenced after the war at Epinay but in 1935 production ceased.

The success of Gallé's venture brought many followers and imitators; some, like the Daum brothers of Nancy, producing work of almost identical design. In cameo glass Daum prefer a mottled or streaky background to Gallé's opaque monotones and smaller Daum pieces such as scent-bottles and miniature vases show very fine enamelling and gilding. The signature 'Daum, Nancy' incorporates the Croix de Lorraine. Gallé's concept of signing his work was eagerly copied by followers everywhere, and this presents an added incentive for the collector of *art nouveau* (plate facing p. 145).

Joseph Brocard, who had exhibited glass at the 1867 World Exhibition, attempted a revival of the exquisite enamelling found on early Islamic glass (plate facing p. 145). He was wholly successful but his later work was influenced by Gallé and Rousseau (1827–91) and began to show a more experimental and individual style in moulded glass, with enamelled formal plant designs of pleasing, but restrained colour. Very little of the work of Eugène Rousseau, one of the earliest glass artists, is definitely identifiable. This artist applied both cased glass and enamelling techniques, and during the early period an oriental influence is very marked. Most impressive are the heavy, sculptured pieces inlaid with glass in a variety of subtle colours, with ingenious surface effects obtained by crackling, metallic inclusions or several other methods. Upon Rousseau's retirement the work was carried on by a pupil, Léveillé, under the name Léveillé-Rousseau. Léveillé's clever colour effects and his crackle glass in sculpturally moulded form gained considerable interest and output was on a sufficient scale for the collector occasionally to come across some of his pieces.

The ancient technique of working with glass paste, *pâte de verre*, was revived in France by Henri Cros toward the end of the nineteenth century and from around 1900 a few artists made use of this medium, which forms a bridge between glass and pottery and has a faint, pleasing translucency. Among the more familiar names associated with *pâte de verre* are those of Dammouse, Décorchemont, G. Argy Rousseau and Almeric Walter. The last is best known to collectors of modern glass for his studies of the dancer, Loïe Fuller, in strong yellow and lime shades.

René Lalique (1860–1945), who studied at the Ecole des Arts Décoratifs, found early success as designer of exclusive jewellery, and working with coloured enamels and glass pastes attracted him to the glass material itself. Lalique's first commercial success was assured with the manufacture of originally designed perfume flasks ordered by Monsieur Coty, and in 1921 the factory at Wingen-sur-Moder was established. The glass of Lalique owes little to the colour effects made so popular during the *art nouveau* period. He relied on form and texture to create their own effect and

Bohemian Zwischengold beaker of the mid-18th century with faceted sides. The inner glass is decorated with a coloured scene on a silver background and the base with a silver vase of flowers on a gilt ground. Ht. 9·2 cm.

A pair of Bohemian/German salt cellars, the bases painted with portraits on red glass medallions with cut and gilded border. The glass is moulded, with additional cutting; *c.* 1800. Size: 8 × 6·5 cm.

Heavily cut and engraved Bohemian crystal vase. The amber-flashed panel has wheel-engraving, probably executed by K. Pfohl during the second half of the 19th century. Ht. 13 cm.

Bohemian thick crystal glass wine decanter with pink and yellow stain and painted decoration of flowers and ornamental scroll work in gilt and silver, c. 1850. Ht. 18·5 cm.

experiments with surface treatment by acid or sandblasting resulted in the subtly frosted, opalescent glass associated with Lalique, which is still produced today. A further typical Lalique creation is a crystal glass with an interior cloudy effect, which reveals a pale ochre tinge when held against the light. It had always been Lalique's aim to exploit the luminous properties of his metal to the fullest and consequently the proportion of coloured glass, in particular opaque coloured glass, is relatively small. Lalique was one of the first men to exploit the possibilities of artistic glass in the field of architecture and he aimed at creating a glass form which would contribute to the aesthetic development of modern life, without losing its sculptural or luminous character. Lalique's treatment of plant and animal forms is based on the concept of geometrical pattern and stylized design, but a trend shared with many of the *art nouveau* artists is shown in ornamental glass exploiting various aspects of the female form. The commercial success was enormous and since Lalique glass was produced by the moulding process it was not difficult to satisfy demands from all over the world. During the late 1920s and the 1930s toilet and table glassware was manufactured in large quantities and artistic individuality conceded to public taste. Lalique is always signed by moulding or acid etching and prior to about 1930 the signature is engraved and the catalogue number of the piece is added. After the death of René Lalique in 1945 the initial R. was omitted from the signature. A few pieces may be numbered up to ten but these were unique early studies and are exceedingly rare. Lalique, too, had its imitators, and frosted glass became extremely popular; a sickly green or pink version was manufactured in large quantities during the 1930s.

Both the factories of Lalique and Daum produce excellent artistic glass today. Lalique still manufacture pieces based on some of the designs popular during the 1920s but they also make table-glass in fine-quality crystal. Daum specialize in crystal of flowing, sculptured form, and a small quantity of coloured and acid-etched glass is also made at this factory.

The glass of Maurice Marinot (1882–1960) is the result of traditional, individual studio work, based on an artistic concept almost ahead of our time. Marinot was painter turned glassmaker and this talent is concentrated in the enamelled decoration found until about 1922, when a certain classical style akin to Picasso's work of the same period is quite distinctive. Marinot not only designed his glass but also made every piece himself, beginning with the process of blowing at the furnace and etching his name on the base after completion. His early approach soon changed to an expressionist treatment of the glass metal itself which he worked into abstract forms and designs of striking impact. His preferred glass metal is heavy and massive, and deeply incised patterns were effected by acid treatment. The often somewhat crude aspect is relieved by inlaid colours and air bubbles, which imbue the mass with a compelling vitality. Such effects, which combine brute force with visual beauty, appeal perhaps more to the modern collector than any other art glass produced in our time.

Spain

Glassmaking began in Spain during the Roman occupation but from its early stage the home industry was exposed to influences as opposed as East and West, and a characteristic Spanish glass art was slow to develop. Design and decorative style oscillate between the Islamic and the Venetian and during the sixteenth century the Venetian influence becomes predominant. Exquisite enamelling, often in characteristic colours of green and white incorporating gilding is associated in particular with Barcelona. The enamelling produced in Cataluña province seems a little more crude but the Catalans were accomplished glass blowers and Venetian latticinio techniques were most successfully applied in that area. A typical form of decoration practised during the sixteenth century in Barcelona and Cataluña is the application of trailed on, opaque white cords. Latticinio glass achieved great popularity and was still made in the eighteenth century. The quality of Spanish metal is poor and rather bubbly, with a greenish tone prevailing during the seventeenth and eighteenth centuries. Crystal glass tends to adopt a grey tone at this time.

Alongside sophisticated techniques a type of rustic glass art developed which delighted in trailed and applied decoration. Stringing, prunting, pinching and trailing produced fanciful and amusing shapes reminiscent of the work of Syrian gaffers. The *almorrata* (a sprinkler), the *cantir* (a water vessel resembling an elegant footed teapot), the long-spouted wine carafe known as *porrón*, as well as oil lamps and wall fonts are the type of domestic glassware subjugated to this fashion. Southern Spain produced much of this exuberant glassware and although a similarly decorated product was manufactured in Cataluña the most impressive pieces must be attributed to Granada.

Engraved decoration is rare in early Spanish glass and was not applied in quantity until after the establishment of the Royal Factory of La Granja de San Ildefonso, founded by a Catalan glassmaker in 1728. Workers from all over Europe came to the factory for short periods and window glass, mirrors and chandeliers were produced in large quantities for the Royal Palace. Typical of the crystal glass produced there are vessels with engraved and firegilt decoration. These date from about 1760 onward but most of the existing specimens were made during the last quarter of the century. The decorative motif consists of repetitive floral design and the craftsmanship seems a little naïve but, on the whole, glass from this factory is pleasing to the eye with its simple, harmonious shapes (plate facing p. 81). Milk glass and opaque coloured glass were produced and attractive mottled effects were achieved with blue splashes on white and vice versa. The Royal Factory also applied colour enamelling to its glassware. In this type of decoration the floral motif is again predominant, but in contrast to engraved and gilded work the enamelled product assumes a cheerful, provincial character. A similar development is apparent in Hungarian glass of the same periods. Here, too, we find eighteenth-century vessels with elaborate applied decoration and some of the enamelling on clear glass shows similar floral motifs.

Glassmaking at the lamp was equally enjoyed by the Spaniard and little figures similar to Nevers appear as early as the sixteenth century.

Russia

Russia, too, is a country that stands between two worlds and has never produced a successful glass art of her own. During the period in which the

Italian Renaissance movement swept over Europe and generated a blossoming of artistic ingenuity and craftsmanship, Russian cultural and artistic life came to a standstill under Mongol occupation. Glass factories were extant in Kiev and Kostroma during the early Christian periods but they were destroyed. In 1637 a Swedish glassmaker, Elias Koet, obtained permission for the establishment of a factory at Mozhaisk; in 1668 another was opened at Izmailova near Moscow with the aid of Italian workmen and by the end of the century glass was manufactured inside the Kremlin walls. By 1717 Peter the Great had founded his Imperial Factory just outside Moscow, on Sparrow Hill, and this establishment was amalgamated with a large glasshouse operating at Yambourg. The glasshouse formed by these two companies was transferred to St. Petersburg about the middle of the century and the factory extended by the addition of experimental workshops. From this time onward glass was made almost exclusively for the Court resulting not only in total commercial failure but prevention of any real progress of the glassmaking industry in other parts of the Russian Empire. Under Elizaveta Petrovna, an academician, Professor M. V. Lomonosov was put in charge of the St. Petersburg glassworks with the aim of making glass *à la façon de Venise*. The only successful work done, however, were some mosaics, including a portrait of Peter the Great completed in 1757. Catherine the Great ennobled one of her more succesful glassmakers, Maltzev, and she bought the Manufacture Impériale de Cristal from Prince Potemkin. Again glass was made exclusively for the Empress's household and any prospect of commercial success was doomed. A few enamelled and dated vessels exist which are decorated in the style of the seventeenth-century German Humpen, but these flasks and pitchers were all made during the eighteenth century.

One of the most gifted Russian glassmakers was Bakhmetev, who established a factory during the early 1760s. Fine enamelling and gilding in the Continental Rococo tradition was ably accomplished at this glassworks and after 1763 every piece was marked. The St. Petersburg factory also produced glass in Continental style. Some of the enamelled milkglass, and a blue glass decanter at the Hermitage decorated in gilt and silver, might have come straight from Bristol. Glass made at St. Petersburg may be signed, amusingly, 'S.P. Burg' in cyrillic lettering. The chandeliers, torchères, vases and goblets made for the Court during the Adam and Regency periods are indistinguishable from luxury glass seen at Potsdam or Versailles. During the nineteenth century the Maltzev glassworks concentrated on domestic ware while Bakhmetev still manufactured costly art glass. Bakhmetev closed down during the Revolution but the works have now been modernized and resurrected under the name of 'Krasniy Gigant'—'Red Giant'. (Plate facing p. 120.)

Glass is used extensively in Russian architecture today and modern glass art strives to achieve an impressive, monumental style.

China

From the evidence of glass beads found in tombs it appears that the Chinese were conversant with glassmaking techniques since the fourth or third century B.C., if not earlier, but it is doubtful whether glassblowing was known before the fifth century A.D.

The earliest surviving glass in good condition dates from the K'ang Hsi period (1662–1722) and from this it is evident that a variety of techniques were successfully applied at the factory in Peking, which came under royal patronage in 1680. The factory produced clear and opaque glass in many colours, in particular a beautiful rich midnight blue, which was applied to vases and bowls. The technique of mould casting was well understood and other forms of decoration included shallow engraving at the wheel, cameo cutting, and enamelling in translucent colours. The defect of crizzling was not overcome until later in the eighteenth century and glass from the early K'ang Hsi period still shows this glass disease. The exquisite snuff-bottles in coloured and cut overlay glass date from the Ch'ien Lung period (1735–95). Striking colour effects are achieved in these miniature masterpieces, which inspired and stimulated Emile Gallé in his own artistic concept of cameo glass when he visited the South Kensington Museum (now the Victoria and Albert Museum) in 1872. An unusual dark-red colour, known as the *sang-de-boeuf*, which is also applied in pottery ware, appears at this time and is found in moulded or carved bowls and vases. Imitation stone glass similar to the Venetian Schmelz was produced during the nineteenth century at Kuantung and Shanting and small animal or vegetable shapes were made from the eighteenth century onward in jewel-like colours of glowing red and blue, commonly termed 'Mandarin glass'.

Fundamentally the Chinese craftsman did not consider glass as a material in its own right but as an additional media to which existing artistic techniques could be applied. A similar approach is apparent in Japanese glass art with often identical results. Enamelling and cloisonné techniques were practised in both countries and objects of enamel or *pâte de verre* were produced in a most accomplished fashion in *plique à jour*, whereby colours of pattern are kept apart by a thin outline of metal strip and the backing removed to achieve translucency. Some of the finest work in *plique à jour* and silver was accomplished by craftsmen in eighteenth- and nineteenth-century Russia.

Contrary to what we might expect from a people who produced the finest and most delicate porcelain, Chinese glass is usually thick and relatively heavy. It is of smooth texture and somewhat oily to the touch, and edges are frequently ground (plate facing p. 144).

Scandinavia

From archeological finds of beads and vessels it is apparent that glass was known in the Scandinavian regions since the early Christian era. Italian glassmakers who reached Scandinavia during the sixteenth century left little trace of their work. The Kungsholm Glasbruk factory was established at Stockholm by Giacomo Scapitta in 1676 and remained in operation until 1815. The Venetian-inspired, thin blown shapes of the early period gave way to more sturdy forms, when cutting and engraving, initiated by German craftsmen, necessitated a more suitable glass metal. Similarly to Russia, the tendency was toward a sophisticated luxury article, since glass was made in large quantities for the royal household. The initials of the reigning monarchs, Charles XI (1655–97) and Charles XII (1697–1718), are incorporated in stems and finials of goblets the pattern of which can be matched in English glass of the same period. Eighteenth-century wines with funnel bowls and twist stems are based on English design and techniques. Graceful chandeliers and epergnes, as well as table candelabra, were destined for the dwellings of the nobility but smaller factories also produced less sophisticated table-ware for average household requirements.

The Norwegian factory established at Nøstetangen in 1741 was the first to operate in the Danish-Norwegian Kingdom under its patron Christian VI of Denmark and Norway. German glassblowers were engaged to work at the Nøstetangen factory and in 1754 a Dane, Morten Waern, was sent to England with the express purpose of studying the composition and manufacture of English lead crystal. He returned in 1755 after many difficulties not only with the requested information but also also with two Newcastle crystal blowers, James Keith and William Brown. In this way the sole Venetian influence to affect Norwegian glassmaking arrived in adulterated form and an Anglo-Venetian glass style appeared in Norway at a time when it was outmoded by some forty years in England. Goblets and bowls, with or without covers, engraved in German style but of Anglo-Venetian design, as well as wines with baluster or twist stems in good-quality crystal came from the Nøstetangen glassworks. By 1757 two further glasshouses were in production; the Hurdals Verk which specialized in crown glass manufacture, apart from attractively decorated ornamental glass, and the Hadeland factory which concentrated on bottle glass. Nøstetangen was enlarged and a great quantity of cheaper and of luxury glass with excellent engraved decoration was produced. Several accomplished glass engravers worked for Nøstetangen. The most important of these was Heinrich Gottlieb Köhler, a German, whose engraving in the Rococo manner equals the best work in the Bohemian tradition (plate facing p. 96). Villas Vinter, who worked with Köhler, has not the same fluidity of style and his artistic approach is more austere. This softens later on when Nøstetangen closed down in 1777 and all artists worked on their own account. More typical of Rococo charm is the glass engraved by Johann Albrecht Becker, a Saxonian who made himself independent in 1773 with a workshop and an established glass trade in Bragernes. Venetian influence comes to the fore in some impressive Nøstetangen chandeliers, which incorporate hollow, mould-blown drops with added wrythening, and where coloured glass produces an additional, Italianate effect. During the late eighteenth century, with the revival of a classical style, coloured, clear and opaque glass began to appear in simple and attractive shapes. The stemmed goblets are replaced by thicker and more squat glasses and beakers. Opaque white and opaque blue glass belong to the Empire and Biedermeier periods and are among some of the most attractive and well-balanced products of Norway's glass industry. The Nøstetangen tradition was continued at Hurdals Verk and in 1808 Hurdals production was taken over by the Gjovik glass factory. A distinctive, deep-blue glass appears after 1808 and is associated with this factory. Enamelled decoration appears less popular than on the Continent. The Royal Cipher occurs frequently, but in itself is no indication of actual age of the object, and most of the spirit flasks decorated in this manner date from the nineteenth century.

The artistic style developed in modern Scandinavia reflects perfectly the contemporary mood of beauty achieved by purity of line and simplicity of form. Much work has been invested in research and some of the most distinctive glass today is produced in Sweden. The Orrefors factory is foremost in artistic glass manufacture and a variety of complicated techniques are applied to objects of clear, simple colour. The Kosta factory, in existence since 1742, produces glass on similar lines. Modern Norwegian glassmaking is concentrated at the factory of Hadeland and the Norsk Glassverk at Mangor. Decorative glass of all kinds is developed with inlaid colours and original surface textures, and in this way subtle effects are achieved.

5
Trends and Possibilities of Today

Economic instability and currency fluctuations are largely responsible for the growing boom in the art market. As demand increases, supplies become more scarce and frequently rare items change hands more than once during relatively short periods. In consequence prices may double in a brief span of time.

During the last few years antique markets have mushroomed in and around large cities. Transactions often take place among the traders themselves, who will advise each other on a variety of business aspects, and the general air of bonhomie is inducive to the collector who desires to explore undisturbed. The large auctioneers hold specialized glass sales and here we find definitely a dealer's market, where the bulk of the best lots offered will go to the big dealers. A particularly reasonable item may be displayed in the showroom at twice its original auction price. On the other hand, the dealer is limited by the amount of profit he can reasonably expect and the private buyer may still obtain a bargain; moreover, he will have the satisfaction of knowing that he has obtained a piece worth having. After all, it is the unpredictable element that creates most excitement in the auction room and if you are unable to attend a sale yourself, your dealer will bid for you, or you may try to place a bid with the auctioneers themselves, provided they are satisfied with your credentials. A tray of oddments often provides just the one piece you have been searching for, and country auctions as well as provincial shops will prove interesting, although the latter are usually well conversant with 'city prices'.

The price survey based on the 1968 Sotheby Index shows an 8½ times rise in glass prices between 1951–68, with the maximum increase of 40 per cent during the season January–July 1968 as against 1967. It must be taken into consideration, however, that this particular period saw the four-part sale of the Walter F. Smith Collection, one of the finest to have come under the hammer for many years. It included the celebrated Applewhaite-Abbot colour twist candlestick sold for £1,350 (as against £110 in 1952), an Innsbruck diamond-engraved and gilded covered goblet (*Vasenpokal*) of 1580 sold for £4,400, and a Nürnberg goblet engraved by Hermann Schwinger, which fetched £1,900. Some exceptionally fine glass was seen in the London auction rooms during the last two seasons and the following prices were obtained for some of the rarer items: an early-sixteenth-century enamelled glass goblet, £500; a late-seventeenth-century Ochsenkopf Humpen, £420; a stippled glass, probably by Wolff, £540; a Kothgasser beaker, £400; a Schaper glass, £320; a rare Jacobite portrait glass, £1,100; a Non-such Bristol blue and gilt finger bowl, £140; a Webb's cameo vase, £500. These are perhaps extreme cases in which provenance plays a weighty role. Kothgasser beakers have been sold during the same season for £40 and Jacobite portrait glasses fetched anything between £70 and £400. In 1912 prices for Jacobite portrait glasses ranged between £5 and £40. By investing in 1912 a sum of £20 at the conservative interest rate of 4½ per cent. the original amount will have increased today by about nine times. This would allow for a glass sold in 1912 for £15 to be purchased today for a sum of £135—a perfectly realistic figure. Certain sections of glass have risen more steeply in price than others, and to these belong engraved and commemorative glasses of any kind. Good drinking glasses incorporating enamel- or air-twists have always been expensive collectors' items but the early group of 'flowered' glasses, that is to say drinking glasses with shallow engraving representing garlands and festoons, seem less popular. The last few years have seen a growing interest in coloured and enamelled glass and this embraces all phases of Continental glassmaking.

The most phenomenal rise in prices has occurred in the two very different categories of French paperweights, on the one hand, and glass of the *art nouveau* period on the other. Neither price level seems truly justified but beauty lies in the eye of the beholder and the true collector will indulge in that which affords the greatest pleasure, provided his purse allows. Paperweights are priced on the basis of rarity of design. They are gay and—an important point—of convenient size, and can, therefore, be easily and attractively displayed. They are also fairly resistant to damage and are usually found in perfect condition. Paperweights seem to hold a special appeal for the male collector and the same observation holds good for *art nouveau* glass. The large amount of material published on the *art nouveau* phase has had an enormously stimulating effect on the collector, who is now much more discerning in his choice. A vogue exists for anything that bears a signature and particularly high prices are asked for French, signed glass. Much of this glass, which may be painted, enamelled or coloured, is very inferior indeed, quite on a par with the hideous imitations of 'Mary Gregory' glass produced in late-Victorian England.

Early Venetian enamelled glass and latticinio glass, sixteenth- and seventeenth-century Continental enamelled glass, eighteenth-century English glass decorated by the Beilbys, or by Edkins, all these belong to the glass aristocracy and are out of reach of the average collector's purse. This also applies to pre-Ravenscroft and especially Ravenscroft sealed pieces, which may realize anything from £1–2,000 upward. In 1960 a unique goblet with a small seal bearing the letter 'S', signifying perhaps the Savoy glasshouse of Hawley Bishopp, was sold for £1,350. However, the proportion of lucky finds is quite high and the beginner collector must not be discouraged. A few years ago a Ravenscroft bowl, discovered in the mud of the Thames, was sold later for around £2,000, and a recent find was a charming, early-eighteenth-century wineglass of drawn trumpet bowl type with shallow, flowered engraving. It had a chip on the conical foot and was of the typical, dark-coloured metal associated with the period. This glass, which would not disgrace any collection of eighteenth-century drinking glasses, was bought for 1s. 6d.

It should be remembered that the decorative techniques of cutting, engraving and enamelling, as well as opaque and colour twists, were applied also to objects other than drinking glasses. Patch stands (plate facing p. 73), candlesticks, taper-sticks, cruets and lacemaker's lamps in which a glass globe is filled with water to condense the light, will incorporate features which may make a drinking glass very expensive indeed but which can be found in a humbler object at considerably lower price. Colour twists, which occur most frequently in the red and opaque variety, are also found in soda glass of the time. They were manufactured in large quantities on the Continent, probably in Holland, and consequently are not as expensive as the English lead crystal glass. A study of soda glass may prove rewarding and collectors specializing in this field may have a chance of picking up some very early glass. Friggers, the small glass toys made by the gaffer during his idle moments, scent-bottles and ink-wells are miniature representatives of their periods and may be easily accommodated and displayed. Additional desirable features, such as attractively worked metal mounts, make collections of these smaller objects particularly interesting and attractive and will help to attribute definite dating. However, care must be taken that the boot fits and the mount is the original one. Missing mounts are replaced much in the same way as bottle tops and decanter stoppers. As a rule the substitute is inferior to the original but occasionally a silver mount may be considerably older than the glass of which it is supposedly a part. A great variety of decanter stoppers were in fashion during the later eighteenth and early nineteenth century and this may make the choice of a replacement somewhat difficult. Bristol decanters and sauce bottles are often found without their original stoppers, which may have been of the flat disc type incorporating lunar sliced cutting and gilding, popular from about 1770 into the early nineteenth century. Irish decanters of the late eighteenth century were made with characteristic, mushroom-shaped stoppers. When in doubt the collector must study existing complete specimens, which are found in museums and good antique shops, and match his stopper accordingly.

Cut glass of the Anglo-Irish period can still be obtained at very little cost. The mode of cutting and the colour of the metal should help the collector in discriminating between the late Victorian product and the Georgian or Regency. During the 1920s a fair amount of faked cut glass came on the market, mostly imported from the Continent. The quality of this glass is good and the most satisfactory way of dealing with it is to compare the doubtful piece with a genuine specimen of the period.

Claret jugs in dark brown, green or reddish bottle glass may still be obtained for about £3–6 each but there again the complete bottle with metal-mounted stopper is difficult to find. Sealed bottles are becoming more expensive and early eighteenth-century specimens, in particular when the original owner can be identified, may reach the £50 mark or more. The slightly later, tall, shouldered bottle can usually be obtained for a few pounds and even the very early, dumpy type may be purchased for around £10–15.

Ancient and oriental glass is not included in specialized glass sales but belongs to the sections classified as antiquities, or Islamic or Oriental art. This in itself makes conditions favourable for spotting and obtaining a bargain, since directly competing buyers probably do not attend in large numbers. The collector of antique glass will obviously have a good chance of making a worth-while purchase when travelling in countries covering those areas where glassmaking was first inspired. Ancient glass sites are continuously rediscovered and explored, and a visitor to Palestine may literally find treasures in the sand. I know of a family living in Israel who have built up a rockery in their garden with most fascinating ancient glass fragments dug up on the plot. Beads are among frequent finds and make a most interesting and useful collection. These earliest representatives of glass art incorporate nearly all techniques known to us today. Odd beads may be bought for very little and make fascinating study. Small Roman glass phials (unguentaria or tear-bottles) are still sold for just a few pounds and many of these rather solid little objects show an attractive iridescence. It has already been pointed out that they should not be confused with Tudor medicine bottles which may have equally attractive iridescence but entirely different, recognisable features. Medical glass as a whole is a somewhat neglected field. Glass utensils have been used by the medical and pharmaceutical professions since antiquity and apart from bottles, a variety of vessels of medical interest may attract the glass collector. Funnels and retorts with straight or curved necks were essential implements for pouring or transferring liquids. Pestles and mortars made of waldglas were certainly in use during the sixteenth century, and eighteenth-century glass measures were intended not only for the innkeeper but also for the medical and pharmaceutical professions. Eighteenth-century apothecary's jars have a special appeal for the collector, since they are often enamelled and gilded. The jars were displayed in windows and on shelves and the painted decoration would consist of a coat of arms of the Society of Apothecaries or any other emblem associated with the profession or the particular pharmacy to which the containers were supplied.

Vessels used for ritual or religious purposes, such as wall-fonts, holy-water sprinklers and reliquary containers have also been neglected by the glass collector. These often form part of a collection confined to ritual objects. In many cases certain inscriptions or initials, such as 'IHS', signify their purpose. During the later eighteenth century we may find names of the town or holy place inscribed, since such objects were often sold as souvenirs to pilgrims or travellers. Catalan wall-fonts and oil-lamps with characteristic gay enamelling or latticinio stripes belong to this group of glass and are still available at reasonable prices.

Walking-sticks and pipes, trumpets, bells, bugles and rolling-pins decorated with coloured latticinio stripes or in coloured, enamelled glass, are friggers often showing intricate and highly accomplished work. They were manufactured in various areas, particularly at Nailsea, Stourbridge and Bristol. The collector with the smallish purse will find a good deal of enjoyment hunting for these objects which are the result of the gaffer's spare-time amusement. To the same category belong the gaily coloured witchballs and the fisherman's floats in the form of green hollow spheres. Witchballs were painted on the inside but in common with mirror glass they could not be satisfactorily silvered until sometime in the nineteenth century. Like the Continental-inspired Christmas-tree decoration they have a hole or a small neck for inserting a peg or stopper and are hung in windows in the hope of warding off evil spirits. Crystal and mirror gazing have long been indispensable aids to the arts of magic and witchballs seem to combine these two media. The green glass balls which serve as floats for fishing-nets were also regarded with some superstition. An identical ball was usually hung up in the fisherman's cottage by the window.

It was guarded by the family as a spiritual contact with the husband and father often in danger at sea. Glass balls decorated with 'Nailsea' latticinio stripes or loops were also produced, but in smaller quantities. They should be obtainable for no more than a few pounds.

Bohemian glass offers some of the most rewarding possibilities to the collector. Variety is enormous. The Biedermeier period, which began after 1815 and lasted until about 1850, produced some exquisite coloured glass of simple and appealing form. Workmanship is usually very good and the enamelled decoration, which includes a large percentage of gilding, is restrained and tasteful. Egerman's Lithyalin and the finest overlay glass belong to this period. An earlier product are the cut Bohemian salt-cellars which are decorated in the manner of Zwischengold, although much less refined in technique. They constitute one of the most delightful of glass-maker's inspirations and were produced between 1790 and 1820, perhaps even until a little later. Oval in shape and of thickish glass they are moulded in the first instance and then ornamented by cutting, in scalloped design. The base is hollowed beneath and closed again by a tightly fitting disc. As in the Zwischengold beaker this disc is decorated on the upper side. Such salt-cellars were usually made in pairs and the painted decoration represents a miniature portrait of a young man on one and a young woman on the other of the pair. The portraits are always on a red background surrounded by a gilded border. It is possible that they may have been intended as wedding gifts, although occasionally salt-cellars of this type have been found with floral decorated design instead of the miniature portrait. The attraction of these somewhat crudely produced salts is now beginning to be appreciated but unfortunately some of the high prices asked would probably purchase a fine Zwischengold beaker of an earlier period. They are obtainable, however, particularly on the continent where they are less expensive (plate facing p. 128). Riedel's *Annagrün* and *Annagelb* glass also appears on the market from time to time. The characteristic colouring should make these vessels easily recognizable, particularly when gilding is present and the style of cutting agrees with the period.

Painted glass roundels and square panes of stained and engraved glass belong to a further section not yet fully explored by the collector. Coloured glass panels were made in fair quantities in Switzerland and they may be obtained in many cases in shops or markets that do not deal exclusively in glass. Because they are made of smallish pieces they have the additional advantage of being usually found in good condition. Glass panels displayed against transmitted light make a most effective collector's item. Prices depend on size and period and will suit most collectors' pockets.

Glass made at the lamp, as for instance *verre de Nevers*, is another collectable item obtainable at less inflated price. A more aristocratic collection may be formed with oriental snuff-bottles. The carved, overlay type can be very expensive, depending on condition of the glass. It should be noted that all such bottles were originally made with their own stopper, which usually adopts form and colouring as applied to the main body and always has its spoon attached. All too frequently such stoppers are missing or the stopper will not match and is of inferior quality. A perfect and complete specimen will obviously be more costly. A box of glass stoppers is stocked by most glass sellers and a decanter can often be fitted with a matching period stopper without great difficulty. Chinese snuff-bottle tops are frequently irreplaceable. The more modest collector might begin with the snuff-bottle which is painted from the inside, a charming object, very skilfully done and less costly than the eighteenth-century carved specimen. A great number of these bottles were made during the nineteenth century. Some are of little artistic merit and probably date from the beginning of the present century. Collectors will gain much help and information from the book by L. S. Perry, *Chinese Snuff Bottles*, published by Tuttle (Tokio), 1960, and Prentice-Hall, 1961.

The English collector abroad might also look out for good English glass, which is far less appreciated on the Continent. In consequence, prices may be relatively reasonable.

In conclusion, the aspiring collector is advised that the best bargains are often found in the best shops, not at a jumble sale.

inese glass, *left to right,*
ade-green brush-holder
the form of a lotus
wer, *c.* 1900. Ht. 6·5
n.; late-19th-century
uff or medicine bottle
th wheel-engraving on
les and body, and
inted on the inside.
t. 11·5 cm.; late-18th-
ntury cameo-cut snuff-
ttle, the colourless crys-
l glass overlaid in red.
Ht. 6·5 cm.

to right, 19th-century English green blown-glass jug with faint rib moulding and pontil mark with
kick in base. Ht. 7·5 cm.; an English wine or condiment jug in cut and fluted crystal with a
nd-away pontil mark, *c.* 1835. Ht. 16·5 cm.; an English or American lead glass jug pressed in
e-part mould, *c.* 1825. Ht. 12·5 cm.; blue opaline Bohemian jug decorated in silver, *c.* 1825. Ht.
12·5 cm.; French white alabaster glass jug made 1825–30. Ht. 11 cm.

A free-blown engraved glass goblet from the New Bremen Glass Manufactory of J. F. Amelung, Maryland, U.S.A. 1793. Ht. 22 cm.

'Favrile' glass, made by L. C. Tiffany after 1900. Ht. 36·7 cm.

French Art Nouveau glass, *left to right:* Emile Gallé: Cameo vase, acid cut. Engraved signature, *c.* 1900. Ht. 16 cm.; vase in 'verre doublé' black streaks in amber glass matrix, impressed signature, *c.* 1890. Ht. 12 cm.; enamelled flacon in 'clair de Lune' glass, elaborate enamelled signature *c.* 1880. Ht. 10 cm.; enamelled glass ewer, mounted in silver gilt. Engraved signatures, *c.* 1870. Ht. 29 cm. Joseph Brocard: Islamic-style lamp, enamelled in blue and white, and gilded. Signed, *c.* 1878. Ht. 13·5 cm.

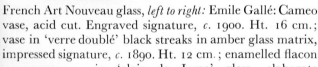

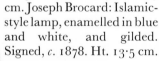

6
Clear as Glass

Thorough knowledge and familiarity with one's glass can be gained only from continuous inspection and handling of specimens, and well-illustrated and documented books are essential in obtaining the necessary background material. A crash-course is no substitute and even an 'infallible instinct' is useless without the necessary experience.

The auction room is still one of the best places for getting to know the field; and glass may be inspected several days prior to being auctioned. Specimens should always be looked at by daylight and the mellow tones of old glass is quite apparent when compared with the bright metal of today. Soda glass may be brownish, yellowish or greenish-grey. It is comparably lighter than lead glass and lacks the typical sparkle of the latter. The characteristic sustained ring associated with glass of lead is missing in soda glass, where the impinged sound stops abruptly. Colour striations may be present due to imperfect decolourizing and pigments, manganese and antimonic acid can be detected by spectral analysis and will help in dating the object. Bubbles and small impurities such as sand specks are usually found in old glass. The typical green tint of the late seventeenth century and the black metal of the early eighteenth century are fair indications of age. The presence of a pontil mark is no true guide but its absence, and a flat, ground base, leaves little doubt as to the object's modernity. In old glass the pontil mark is left rough and may show some black specks. Between 1800 and about 1830 the pontil mark was ground away, leaving a deep, circular impression on the base. Early cut glass will also show a rough pontil mark, unless the base is decorated by cutting. Marks of wear in the form of minute scratches should be observed on all old glass, both under foot and on the rim of wineglasses, which were usually stored upside down. Under the magnifying-glass such scratches should show up running in all directions; several parallel lines may indicate 'touching up' with emery paper. If the object incorporates matt surfaces, these ought to show handling marks. All-important are the proportions of the English drinking glass. Should these be incorrect, then the glass must be considered either a forgery or a foreign-produced specimen. In the English glass the foot has always a slightly larger or at least as large a circumference as the rim of the bowl. The foot, if not domed, should always rise to meet the stem, and the bottom of the bowl should be slightly thickened at the point of contact with the stem. The stem itself, when straight, should feel fairly smooth without narrowing perceptibly between foot and bowl. If the stem encloses a spiral the twist should come to the edge of the stem but should not be felt noticeably when held between the fingers. The twist itself should be even, not too oblique, and run corkscrew-wise from right to left. In common with Bristol opaque white glass, the English opaque twist is of a dense, white colour, whereas the Continental variant has a milk-and-water quality which may show a faint blue or grey tinge. Double ogee bowls are often attributed to Bristol manufacture but twists with exaggerated, waisted bell bowls and much everted lip are usually of Continental make. The lip itself is cut with the shears while the metal is in the plastic stage. The edge should therefore be nicely rounded without too much thickening. Ground or flat lips are signs of either removal of a chip by grinding or spuriousness. The same applies to the edge of the plain foot; a chip in the foot is preferable to a chipped bowl and should be left untouched. Occasionally one comes across some highly accomplished repair work which may defeat even the expert unless he has been warned. If nothing foreign has been added this should not detract too much from the value of the object. It is a different story when a coaching glass, which is made to rest upside down, sports a heavy foot, or an eighteenth-century Bohemian engraved goblet is adorned with a stem and foot which sparkles with ornate, prismatic cutting of the nineteenth century.

When a genuinely old glass has been engraved at a much later date, and this is all too often the case, expert advice may be necessary. White paper or a white handkerchief will show up the colour of the metal; a white handkerchief placed inside the bowl of the questionably engraved glass may prove helpful. If the engraved part appears very much lighter than the rim of the bowl it is likely that it has been added later. Traces of rouge powder or emery, applied to 'age' the engraving, will show up under the lens. Because of their great desirability and high price Jacobite glasses are typical victims of the later engraver. The most dominant form of decoration encountered in Jacobite glasses is the air-twist, of which the earliest type is the drawn trumpet, which may be engraved with a variety of typical emblems such as the rosebud and the word 'FIAT'. Portrait glasses never incorporate trumpet bowls and although there are exceptions to every rule these have to be considered from all angles and it is unlikely that the portrait of Bonnie Prince Charlie engraved on a drawn trumpet is as old as the glass itself. Indeed, the entire specimen may be spurious. However, Irish Williamite glasses may show portraits on trumpet bowls.

Mixed colour twists, especially red and white, and green, were made in great quantities during the nineteenth and early twentieth century and were mostly imported from Bohemia and Holland. It is therefore advisable to be particularly careful when purchasing colour spirals and to pay special attention to all relevant features. Air-twists are copied less frequently since they are more difficult to manufacture but spurious cut stems and cut glasses are produced in quantity, although modern cutting results in sharper angles.

Enamelled glass, in particular the German and Bohemian Humpen type, was copied in large numbers on the Continent during the later nineteenth century. Much of this painted decoration was originally carried out by the cold enamelling technique, and colour application therefore presents no particular difficulties. However, the actual work is too smooth and skilful to be mistaken for sixteenth- or seventeenth-century work and the glass metal itself is usually of a very prominent and even, greenish tone, which can in no way be mistaken for the early blown glass with its blemishes and faint colour tinge. Saracen enamelled glass is almost impossible to find on the open market and here any object offered must be viewed with suspicion. In the modern forgery the cold applied paint or lacquer may be easily scraped off. Tours de force, as are the Zwischengold beakers and cameo glass, are less often faked. They are far too intricate and difficult to produce and rarely appear a financial proposition. Spurious painted or stained glass is usually detected by the arrangement and attitude of the figures represented and by the use of incorrect, more modern colour pigments.

Early mirrors will have been made by the broad sheet technique and will therefore show certain irregularities which do not occur in the plate-glass product manufactured first in France (1688) and by 1773 in England. Mirror glass produced by the blown broad sheet method is much thinner than the later plate-glass. During the eighteenth century the metal foil backing was achieved by the use of tin foil coated with mercury but in the mid-nineteenth-century a new development resulted in the application of a reddish brown lead oxide coating on top of the silvering, in order to prevent corrosion.

Some very good 'old' glass has been and is being produced in Italy. Paperweights are particularly well done and attention must be paid to colour and wear marks. Czechoslovakia has recently recommenced the manufacture of beautiful ruby-flashed and engraved glass based on designs and forms of their finest eighteenth- and nineteenth-century work. This is exported in good faith as new glass but it may be found in antique shops. It is much lighter in weight than its early prototype and, unless it has been deliberately mistreated to look old, will not deceive the careful collector.

Candelabra and chandeliers may have had parts replaced at one time or other. Certain glass shops specialize in stocking old crystal drops but it is not always possible to find a period piece which matches exactly. Modern imitations abound and if an entire object is made up of a variety of non-matching parts it is best left alone.

Iridescent glass has been faked in a number of ways. It may be made of re-melted modern iridescent glass, a method which would require workshop conditions, or it may be treated by aniline dyes applied to a previously roughened surface. Another method is to painstakingly apply iridescent flakes obtained from genuine, ancient fragments. Enamelled and iridescent forgeries are usually coated with some fixatives such as high-gloss resins or synthetic films, all of which are pervious to certain solvents; often mere washing will reveal the spuriousness.

When in doubt, discussion with fellow collectors will generally prove fruitful. Museum staff today are busier and more active than they have ever been and should not be burdened with trivialities which can be resolved elsewhere. However, provision has been made at some museums for enquiries to be dealt with at specified times.

TERMINOLOGY

To include a list of all terms used in describing the features of glass would only confuse the beginner, particularly since 'glass language' is by no means standardized—as yet. Even the simple descriptive term of 'knop' may be found as 'knob'. Opaque white glass is variously described as 'milk glass'—the Italian lattimo—or as 'enamel glass', and latticinio decoration may be referred to as 'filigree' glass. Such and similar terms have been explained in the text and will be found duly indexed. The following glossary includes terms and subjects not referred to in the main chapters, or which have not been fully explained and may not be found in any general concise dictionary.

Ale Yard or Yard-of-Ale Glass: a long glass used for special occasions and as a trick glass. The shape is derived from the coach horn. Ale yards have a long, trumpet-shaped funnel with a bulbous end. They are not designed to stand and the drinker must empty the glass with care or else the liquid will spurt into his face. Half yards were also made.

Battledore: a flat, long, wooden tool used to flatten the base of glass objects.

Booze Bottles: American. Made in 1860 by the Whitney Glass Works for Edmund G. Booz of Philadelphia, and intended for whisky.

Bumping Glass: firing glass.

Case Bottles: four-sided bottles made to fit into compartments of cases or boxes. Often supplied with ornamental silver tops which facilitate dating.

Cider Glasses: flute-shaped glasses which may be engraved with emblems denoting contents, i.e. fruiting apple-tree or, in the case of ale, hops and barley. The Scudamore or Chesterfield flute at the London Museum is the most famous English cider glass.

Clock Lamps: in principle, a table standard oil lamp made of metal, usually brass. The oil is poured into a glass container mounted in brass and marked by hour degrees. Popular from just before 1800 in this form.

Coaching Glass: a regency flute, cut and without foot, a short thick cut stem ending usually in a heavy knop, often also cut. Its purpose was for the coachman and the travellers to take their wine at a wayside inn, without leaving the vehicle, the wine being brought to them and the glasses emptied and stood upon the tray upside down. It is possible, however, that these now rare glasses were carried by the travellers themselves, perhaps slipped inside a ring or bracket fixed to the interior walls of the coach.

Cockle: Wavy lines formed by contracting glass.

Coin Glass: a wineglass, goblet or tankard enclosing a coin in the hollow knop of stem or foot. Popular from the latter half of the seventeenth century onward, although the British Museum collection possesses a Venetian glass with coin dated 1647. Pro- and anti-Jacobite sympathies were supposedly expressed by using coins portraying either Charles II or monarchs of the House of Hanover.

Cranberry Glass: glass of a pinky-red colour, popular during the later Victorian period, and often decorated with so called 'Mary Gregory' children in white or pinkish enamel.

Crimping: process of forming wavy or fluted edges, e.g. in *façon de Venise*.

Door Stops: also referred to as bottle-green paperweights. Produced in most glassmaking areas but larger and heavier than the glass paper-weight. The metal is common bottle glass with interior decoration of bubbles, often in the shape of plants or fountains. The ornamental pattern was obtained by sprinkling chalkpowder on to the marver in the shape of the required design and pressing the plastic ball of glass on to it. This process was repeated on successive layers until the glass weight had obtained the desired size. The heat released by the glass caused the entrapped chalk particles to emit gases which form clouds of silvery bubbles in the shape of the original chalk pattern.

Gimmel or Gimmal Flask: double flask pourable from one side without disturbing the other.

TERMINOLOGY

Hour Glass or Sand Glass: the timing device popularized in the egg-timer and used as early as the eighth or ninth century. The frame is of more interest than the glass and may be made of carved ivory, wood or bone.

Insufflated: American term used to denote 'contact three-section blown mould' glass, i.e., glass blown into a three-sectional mould.

Jelly Glasses: small glasses with bowl set directly on to the foot, usually having one handle. The handle-less type is similar to the Hogarth glass in shape and was made from after 1745. Bowls were largely bell-shaped and often decorated by cutting.

Lime Glass: term denoting American substitute for lead glass developed in 1864 by chemist W. Leighton of the Wheeling Glass Factory, West Virginia. Cools and can be finished more quickly than lead glass; a saving in production costs.

Linen Smoothers: thick glass implement of mushroom shape, the handle about 5 in. long, grooved or knopped to facilitate gripping. May be of coloured bottle glass but was also made in thick, colourless, transparent glass.

Lustre: cut-glass pendant from chandelier. Also ornamental glass candle holder with cut-glass drops sometimes referred to as vase lustre.

Marbles: evolved with the making of beads. Manufactured in Venice in the sixteenth century incorporating all types of latticinio patterns and colours and produced by the same technique. Applied in manufacture of spun glass, which is drawn from individual remelted marbles.

Mascarons or Macaroons: raised, applied ornaments also known as bosses or prunts, but which have masks impressed upon them, as for instance the lion masks on glass *à la façon de Venise*.

Master Glass or Captain: the largest and central piece of a set of sweetmeat glasses. May also refer to the tall glass used by the Worshipful Master of a Company or a Freemason's Lodge.

Mead Glasses: commonly thought to have been of small bowl form, perhaps similar to the mediaeval 'maigelein', but by the mid-eighteenth century footed similar to the Rummer. Not made later than about 1760.

Mule: very occasionally used to describe the foot of a wineglass.

Obsidian: dark vitreous lava or volcanic rock similar to bottleglass. One of the earliest known natural glass-like substances, used for making primitive tools particularly in South American regions, and found in areas such as Mexico.

Pomona Glass: American designation of clear glass produced by expanded mould blowing with subsequent ornamentation by etching or staining. Mainly produced by the New England Glass Company.

Posset Pots: used for serving thick and warm liquids, for instance sillabub. Reminiscent of invalid cups, posset pots have a spout and cover and usually two handles. Some fine examples are extant bearing the Ravenscroft seal.

Potichomanie: derived from the French and denoting type of decoration on glass vases in imitation of porcelain or pottery fashionable during the later nineteenth century.

Rosettes: glass in this form was often attached to metal screws used for supporting mirrors. Also applied in contemporary mirror making.

Rotten Stone: decomposed siliceous limestone used for polishing.

Sillabub Glass: made in a variety of forms, possibly similar to the posset pot and caudle glass, having either one or two handles.

Silvered Glass: the use of silverfoil between glass was known in antiquity and was applied, although rarely, in wineglasses of the pre-Ravenscroft period. Popular silvered glass was produced in England and America from about 1850. The nineteenth-century process consisted of coating thinly blown glass with a silvery substance and covering the coating with a second thin glass layer. A similar effect was achieved by pouring the substance or silver paint into the space between two glass layers through the pontil hole, which was then sealed or plugged up to prevent deterioration of the silver coating.

Sweetmeat Glasses: a stemmed glass with open bowl often described as champagne glass, from which it is in some cases indistinguishable. Most forms of contemporary fashion were applied to sweetmeat glasses, which are usually of very good quality. Frequent features are double ogee bowl, scalloped cut rim and foot, vertical mould ribbing, domed and folded feet. Stems may incorporate spiral twists. They are usually of thicker metal than the ordinary wineglass. The form known to us developed toward the end of the seventeenth century.

Tapersticks: small candlesticks about 5–7 in. high, fashionable during the second half of the eighteenth century. Used for holding tapers.

Toddy Lifters: used for serving punch in the eighteenth and early nineteenth century. About 6 in. high they are of the shape of a tiny decanter, with a long neck about double the height of the body. Toddy lifters are based on the principle of suction, with a small hole in the base. When immersed they fill slowly and the liquid is kept in the container by placing the thumb on the orifice. It is then transferred to the waiting glass. Main form of decoration was by cutting. They appear to be entirely British, or more precisely Scottish, as they are claimed to have been invented in Scotland.

Violin Bottles: American so-shaped bottles made during the nineteenth century in a variety of sizes and colours and in large quantities. Mould blown, usually decorated with emblems of commemorative nature. Jenny Lind bottles belong to this attractive group made during the early 1850s. Much favoured by collectors.

Wineglass Coolers: also referred to as 'monteighs' or 'montiths'. These were filled with cold water and used for cooling wineglasses. Popular during the late eighteenth century but in use a hundred years earlier. Made for two glasses, they were double-lipped to rest the stem of the immersed wineglass, which was placed in the bowl upside down for cooling. Many monteighs were made in Bristol blue glass with gilding, together with matching plate and finger bowl. Large wine (bottle) coolers are also referred to as monteigh bowls.

MUSEUMS AND SPECIAL COLLECTIONS

Even the smallest township will normally possess a museum or gallery of interest to the collector. Areas associated with Roman occupation or glass-making families are continuously explored. Digging up the past has led to many interesting finds and the results of excavations are often displayed in the local museum. Special exhibitions are arranged in most museums from time to time. In connection with the Eighth International Glass Congress held in London in July 1968, special exhibitions were mounted by several museums. The unique collection of the British Museum, which covers all ages and regions of glassmaking history, was brought together for the first time in a single, complete exhibition, instead of being dispersed throughout the entire museum. The Victoria and Albert Museum arranged a special exhibition of English glass which was to a large extent made possible by loan specimens from private collectors, with the distinction of including four Verzelini glasses in addition to the museum's own Barbara Potter glass from Jerome Bowes' glasshouse. Worthing Museum and Art Gallery showed a collection of English drinking glasses. The main core of this exhibition was formed by part of Albert Hartshorne's collection. Catalogues of such exhibitions, when still available, are quite invaluable to the collector and are normally relatively low in cost.

In the following list brief mention is made of some of the specialized sections in a variety of glass collections. It should be understood, however, that most museums cover additional fields which may be of interest to the collector.

London:

Bethnal Green Museum
  Venetian nineteenth-century glass.

British Museum
  Egyptian, Roman, Seine–Rhine, Pre-Islamic, Persian, Mesopotamian, Islamic, Chinese, European glass from Middle Ages to Victorian.

Guildhall Museum
Now re-forming collection in newly erected building. Glass excavated
from the City of London. Fragments and entire specimens dating from
Roman times to eighteenth century.

London Museum
English glass. Building now modernized and collections newly arranged
and well displayed.

Historical Medical Museum of the Wellcome Foundation, Euston Road,
N.W.1
Medical glass.

Science Museum
Wealden glass fragments. Exhibitions of scientifically reconstructed
models and special section on glass history.

Victoria and Albert Museum
European glass. Special sections include oriental snuff-bottles, ancient
glass, stained glass.

Wallace Collection (Hertford House)
Glass in *façon de Venise*.

Accrington
Tiffany glass collection.

Bedford
Cecil Higgins Museum. Seventeenth- and eighteenth-century English
glass. Continental glass including specimens of the famous Miotti
opaque white enamelled glass.

Birmingham Art Gallery
Venetian glass. Lead crystal.

Bournemouth
The Russell-Cotes Art Gallery. A variety of glass, lead crystal and also
a collection of Russian enamelled objects in *plique à jour*.

Brierley Hill (Public Library)
Local nineteenth-century glass.

Bristol City Art Gallery
Decanters from John Bacon Collection. H. R. B. Abbey Collection of Chinese glass. Local coloured glass.

Cambridge
Fitzwilliam Museum. Roman glass. Fine Syrian glass including early-fourteenth-century mosque lamp. Continental glass. English bottles.

Colchester
Pre-Seine–Rhine and Seine–Rhine glass.

Edinburgh
Royal Scottish Museum. Extensive glass collection including *art nouveau.*

Exeter
Royal Albert Memorial Museum. The Henry Hamilton Clarke Collection of English glass.
Historical Museum. English bottles.

Farnham, Dorset
The Pitt Rivers Museum. Ancient glass from the Eastern Mediterranean areas.

Guildford
Wealden glass.

Glasgow Art Gallery and Museum
Antiquities and stained-glass. Continental glass, including Murano and Venetian.

Haslemere
Wealden glass.

Hull
Mediaeval glass and fragments from York.

Leeds City Museum
Roman, Syrian and Near-Eastern Glass.

Leamington Spa
Public Library Art Gallery and Museum. Eighteenth-century English glasses including Lynn and Newcastle decorated wines. *Façon de Venise.* The famous Elgin Vase engraved by John Northwood in 1873.

Lincoln
Usher Art Gallery. The Ruston Collection of European seventeenth-century glass.

Liverpool
Eighteenth-century English glass.

Manchester
City Art Gallery. Lead crystal. Eighteenth-century South Lancashire glass.
University Museum. Syrian, Egyptian and Alexandrian glass from the Flinders Petrie excavations.

Newcastle-upon-Tyne
The Laing Art Gallery and Museum. Local glass. North-Country glass.

Northampton
Central Museum. Seine–Rhine, Anglo-Saxon glass. Eastern snake thread specimens. The earliest intact sealed bottle dated 1657. Lead crystal. Good English and Continental glass.

Norwich Castle Museum
Archaeological glass. Eighteenth-century English glass, in particular work by William Absolon, the Yarmouth gilder and enameller. Lynn glass.

Nottingham Castle Museum and Art Gallery
Eighteenth-century English glass. A fine covered posset pot. Very good specimen of Venetian enamelled early-sixteenth-century goblet.

Oldham
  Municipal Art Gallery. Part collection of Francis Buckley's lead crystal glass.

Oxford
  Ashmolean Museum. Roman glass. English seventeenth- and eighteenth-century glass including fine Jacobite and opaque white enamelled glass. The Marshall collection.
  Pusey House. Not public but may be viewed on special application. The Wiltshire collection of Christian *fondi d'oro* glasses.

Peterborough Museum
  Lead crystal. Glass from Roman Britain.

Sheffield
  Weston Park Museum. Syrian and Near-Eastern glass. English lead crystal. Glass from South Yorkshire area.

St. Helen's
  The Pilkington Glass Museum (near Liverpool). Built by Pilkington Brothers in 1961, this fascinating modern museum is set in the very core of one of the greatest glass-manufacturing centres. The collection represents every phase of glassmaking history and all techniques and developments are illustrated by splendidly effective audio-visual aids.

Taunton
  Somerset County Museum. English bottles, seventeenth/eighteenth century.

Worthing
  Archeological glass, Roman and Anglo-Saxon.

Collections in other Countries

Belgium
  Brussels, Musées Royaux d'Art et d'Histoire.
  Liège. Musée du Verre.

American South Jersey-type pitcher, attributed to the Lancaster or Lockport Glassworks. Non-lead glass, deep aquamarine. Free-blown with applied lily-pad decoration, *c.* 1840–60. Ht. 18 cm.

A lacy-glass cream pitcher from the Fort Pitt Glassworks of R. B. Curling & Sons, Pittsburg, U.S.A. Colourless lead glass, pressed in one piece, *c.* 1829–32. Ht. 11·3 cm.

Lacy-glass plate probably from the Pittsburg area. Colourless, pressed lead glass, *c.* 1830. Dia. 19 cm.

Czechoslovakia
Jablonc, Museum of Glass.
Prague, Museum of Applied Art.
Prague, Museum of Decorative Art.

France
Nancy, Le Musée de l'Ecole de Nancy. (The cradle of *Art Nouveau*).
Paris, Conservatoire National des Arts et Métiers.
       Musée des Arts Decoratifs (Louvre).
       Musée de l'Art Moderne.
       Musée de Cluny.

Germany
Berlin, Kunstgewerbe Museum.
Cologne museums: incomparable collection of Roman/Rhenish glass including diatreta, particularly at the Römisch-Germanisches Museum, Kunstgewerbe Museum.
Darmstadt. Collection of *Art Nouveau* at the Hessisches Landesmuseum.
Hanover, Kestner Museum.
Munich, Bayerisches National Museum.
Nürnberg, Germanisches Museum.

Holland
Amsterdam, Rijksmuseum.

Israel
Jerusalem, the Israel Museum.
Tel-Aviv, fine ancient glass at the Haaretz Museum.

Italy
Murano, Museo Vetrario.
Ravenna, Museo Nazionale.
Venice, Museo Civico Correr.

Spain
Barcelona, Museos de Arte.
Madrid, Museo Arqueologico Nacional.

U.S.A.

New York, the Corning Museum.
Metropolitan Museum of Art.
Philadelphia Museum.
Toledo (Ohio), Toledo Museum of Art.

U.S.S.R.

Leningrad, Hermitage Collection.
Moscow, Historical Museum.

BOOKS FOR FURTHER STUDY AND
BIBLIOGRAPHICAL REFERENCES

Some of the books cited are standard reference works now out of print. They are occasionally obtainable in antiquarian shops and can be reserved and taken out on loan at most good reference libraries.

Arnau, F.
  Kunst der Fülscher de Kunst. Düsseldorf, 1959, Econ Verlag.
Ash, D.
  How to Identify English Drinking Glasses and Decanters, 1680–1830. London, 1962, G. Bell & Sons Ltd.
Barrelet, J.
  La Verrerie en France de l'Epoque Gallo-romaine à Nos Jours, Paris, 1953, Larousse (Arts, Styles et Techniques).
Barrington-Haynes, E.
  Glass Through the Ages, London, 1948, Penguin, 2nd edition 1964.
Bernt, W.
  Altes Glas, Munich, 1947, Prestel Verlag.
Bles, J.
  Rare English Glasses of the 17th and 18th Centuries, London, 1926, Geoffrey Bles.
Boros, B.
  Glassmaking in old Hungary, Budapest, 1963, Corvina Press.
Buckley, F.
  Old English Glass, London, 1925, E. Benn.
Buckley, W.
  European Glass, London, 1926, E. Benn.
  Diamond Engraved Glasses of the Sixteenth Century, London, 1929, E. Benn.
  The Art of Glass, London, 1939, The Phaidon Press.
Dillon, E.
  Glass, London, 1907, Methuen (Connoisseur Library).
Elville, E. M.
  Paperweights and Other Glass Curiosities, London, 1954, Country Life.
Francis, G. R.
  Old English Drinking Glasses, London, 1926, H. Jenkins.
Frothingham, A.
  Spanish Glass, London, 1963, Faber & Faber.
Galliner, A.
  Glasgemälde des Mittelalters aus Wimpfen, Freiburg, 1932, Urban Verlag.
Gasparetto, Astone
  Il Vetro di Murano dalle Origini ad Oggi, Venice, 1958, Arti Grafiche delle Venezie.

Godden, A.
Antique China and Glass Under £5, London, 1966, Arthur Barker Ltd.
Guttery, D. R.
Broad Glass to Cut Crystal, London, 1956, Leonard Hill.
Harrison, F.
Stained Glass of York Minster, London, Studio Publication.
Hartshorne, A.
Old English Glasses, London, 1897, Edward Arnold.
Hettes, Karel.
Glass in Czechoslovakia, Prague, 1958, S.N.T.L.
Honey, W. B.
English Glass, London, 1946, Collins.
Glass, London, 1946, V. & A. Guide.
Hughes, G. B.
English, Scottish and Irish Tableglass, from the 16th century to 1820, London, 1956, Batsford.
Imbert, R. and Amic, Y.
Les Presse-Papiers Français. Paris, 1948, Art et Industrie (French and English).
Jokelson, P.
Antique French Paperweights, New York, 1955.
Sulphides. The Art of Cameo Incrustation, New York, 1968.
Levinson, Ye. A., Smirnov, B. A., Shelkovnikov, B. A., Entyelis, F. S.
Khudozhestvyennoye Steklo i yevo Primenenye v Arkhitekturye (Artistic Glass and its Application in Architecture), Leningrad–Moscow, 1953, State Publishing House for Literature on Building and Architecture.
Maciver, Perceval.
The Glass Collector, London, 1918, Herbert Jenkins.
McKearin, H. and G. S.
American Glass, New York, 1941, Crown Publishers.
Neuburg, F.
Glass in Antiquity, London, 1949, The Art Trade Press Ltd. (Rockcliffe Publ. Corp.).
Ancient Glass, London, 1962, Barrie and Rockliff.
Pazaurek, G. E.
Moderne Gläser, Leipzig, 1901, Hermann Seemann, Nachfolger.
Gläser der Biedermeier Zeit, Leipzig, 1923, Monographien des Kunst Gewerbes, No. 13–15.
Perry, Lilla S.
Chinese Snuffbottles, printed Tokio, 1960, Charles E. Tuttle.
Polak, A.
Gammelt Norsk Glass, Oslo, 1953, Kunstindustri Museet.
Fire Pionerer I Nyere Fransk Glasskunst, Nordenfjeldske Kunstindustrimuseum, Arbok 1956.
Modern Glass, London, 1962, Faber & Faber.

Savage, G.
Forgeries, Fakes and Reproductions, London, 1963, Barrie & Rockliff, Cresset Press.
Schmidt, R.
Das Glas, Vienna, 1922, W. de Gruyter & Co.
Thorpe, W. A.
English and Irish Glass, London, 1927, Medici Society.
A History of English and Irish Glass (2 Vols.), London, 1929, Medici Society.
English Glass, London, 1935, A. & C. Black.
Volf, M. B.
Sklo, Prague, 1947, V. Poláček.
Wakefield, H.
Nineteenth Century British Glass, London, 1961, Faber & Faber.
Westropp, M. S. Dudley.
Irish Glass, London, 1920, H. Jenkins.
Wilmer, D.
Early English Glass, London, 1910, L. Upcott Gill.
Winbolt, S. E.
Wealden Glass, Hove, 1933, Combridges (ed. of 500).
Woodforde, C.
Stained and Painted Glass in England, London, 1937, Society for Promoting Christian Knowledge.

Articles and Papers:
The Connoisseur
    'James Giles as a Decorator of Glass', R. J. Charleston, June and July 1966.
    'Wolff Glasses in an English Private Collection', Hugh Tait, June 1968.
Apollo
    'Poetry in Glass, The Art of Emile Gallé', Gabriella Gros, November 1955.
    '19th Century Cameo Glass', Geoffrey Beard, February 1956.
    'Dutch Engraved Glass in the A. J. Guepin Collection', B. R. M. de Neeve, November 1964.
Antique Dealer and Collector's Guide
    'Bottles of Great Charm', Alister Campbell, September 1954.
    'The Case for Lalique', Gabriella Gros, November 1968.
Journal of Glass Studies, Vol. VIII 1966, Corning Museum of Glass
    'The Egyptian Sand-Core Technique: a New Interpretation', Dominick Labino.
Transactions of the Society of Glass Technology
    'Michael Edkins and the Problem of English Enamelled Glass', R. J. Charleston, Vol. XXXVIII, 3–16, 1954.
    'Dutch Decoration of English Glass', R. J. Charleston, Vol. XLI, 229–43, 1957.

Transactions of the Circle of Glass Collectors
'The Elements of Glass Collecting', John M. Bacon. No. 2
'Verre de Nevers', Mrs. William King. 10
'King's Lynn Glass', Ivan Napier. 29
'Newcastle Glass', Ivan Napier. 39
'More Newcastle Glass', John M. Bacon. 40
'Colour Tints in English Glass', Ivan Napier. 45
'Frans Greenwood and his Glasses', Ivan Napier. 58
'Islamic Contribution to the Art of Glass', R. J. Charleston. 91
'Roman Glass in Britain', Dorothy Charlesworth. 105
'Some Notable Glass on Public View in England',
R. J. Charleston. 107
'The Art of Glass in Hesse-Kassel', F.A. Dreier. 145
'The Apsley Pellatts', J. A. H. Rose. 150
'Scottish Glasshouses', R. Oddy. 151
Silicates Industriels, Brussels, Aug./Sept. 1951
'Note Relative à deux Chefs d'Oeuvre en Verre Fabriqué en Belgique au
milieu de XVIe Siecle', Raymond Chambon.
Connaissance des Arts, No. 102, August 1960 (France)
'Le Cas Etrange de Monsieur Gallé', Helene Démoriane.
Specialized Catalogues and Museum Publications:
British Museum: Masterpieces of Glass (1968 Exhibition).
Victoria and Albert Museum: Circle of Glass Collectors Commemorative
Exhibition 1937–1962. English Glass (1968 Exhibition).
The Metropolitan Museum of Art, New York: Early American Glass, 1940.
The Toledo Museum of Art, Toledo, Ohio:
American Glass.
Early American Pressed Glass.
European Glass.
Ancient and Near Eastern Glass.
New England Glass Company.

SIGNIFICANT DATES

c. 3100 B.C. It may be assumed that glass beads were manufactured at that time, since two beads of blue glass were found among the ruins of the city of Memphis attached to a gold necklace stamped with the name of Menes, first king of the first Egyptian dynasty, reigning from about 3100–3038 B.C.

2600 Glazed pottery wares in Egypt.

1500 Appearance of small glass vessels in Egypt and Syria.

300 Establishment of Alexandrian Glass industry, dominant for over 300 years.

A.D.   1 Discovery of glass blowing, possibly at Sidon.

20 Glasshouses in Italy. Blown glass introduced in Italy.

324 Official adoption of Christianity in Rome. Roman glass finds of this period stretch across the Roman Empire.

475 Fall of the Roman Empire.

500 Glass in China.

600–700 Islam overrun by Arabs who establish distinct Islamic culture.

800–1400 So-called 'empty ages' (in Western glass art).

1000–1100 Venice produces glass beads and small vessels.

1100–1200 York Minster stained glass.

1240 Westminster Abbey stained glass.

1291 Establishment of Venetian glass industry on the island of Murano.

1250–1400 Islam produces its finest enamelled work.

1400 Fall of Damascus.

1400–1500 Venice revives the art of fine enamelling.

1500+ Venice develops a glass of clear, colourless metal—the 'cristallo'.

1507 Dal Gallo of Murano obtains right to manufacture blown mirror glass.

1549 Eight Murano glassworkers arrive in England.

1573 Verzelini establishes his glasshouse in London, where by the year 1589 fifteen glasshouses are in existence.

1615   'Proclamation touching glasses' issued, forbidding use of wood fuel.

1623   Sir Edward Mansell secures patent to manufacture all types glass and begins to reorganize English glass industry.

1635   Charter granted to the London Glass Sellers' Corporation by Charles I.

1635   Mansell begins smelting with ordinary coal.

1637   Re-establishment of glass industry at Mozhaisk, Russia.

1664   Reincorporation of the Worshipful Company of Glass Sellers.

1665   Eighteen Venetian glassworkers arrive in Paris.

1670   Duke of Buckingham founds first factory of blown mirror glass in England at Lambeth.

1676   Ravenscroft's lead glass patented.

1688   Lucas de Nehou invents method of casting and rolling glass at Tours la Ville.

1722   The art of diamond stippling begins to flourish in the Netherlands.

1739   Caspar Wistar's glasshouse established in New Jersey, U.S.A.

1745–6   Tax levied on glass by weight of ingredient (in England).

1777   Second Glass Excise Act, taxing also white enamel glass.

1780   Trade restrictions lifted between England and Ireland.

1825   Excise Duty imposed on Irish Glass.

1827   America develops pressing machine of revolutionary design.

1845   Excise Duty on Glass removed.

INDEX

INDEX

Cameo glass, 48–9, 55, 115–16, 127
Cameo incrustation technique, 40–1
Carder, Frederick, 120
Carré, Jean, 16
Carthage, 13
Casting process, 18, 19, 30, 32
Cataluña, 130–1
Catherine the Great (Empress), 132
Catherine of Braganza, 99
Cellini, Benvenuto, 82
Chance Brothers, 117
Chance, William, 113–14
Chariot cup, 58
Charles I (Eng. k.), 17, 99
Charles II (Eng. k.), 91, 99, 152
Charles XI (Swed. k.), 134
Charles XII (Swed. k.), 134
Charles, Edward, Prince, 147
Chartres, 15, 67
Chemnitz, 27
Cherbourg, 122
Chesterfield flute, 91, 151
China, 21, 70, 127, 133–4
Choisy-le-Roi, 124
Christian VI (Dan. k.), 135
Church, the: glass vessels and, 61; window-glass art and, 15, 22, 66
Cistercian Order, 67
Civico Correr Museum, 73
Claw-beaker manufacture, 60
Clichy, 40, 124–5
Closour, 68
Clouzot, H., 123
Clutha glass, 114
Coal Firing, 17, 97
Coin glass, 152
Collections, *listed geographically*, 156–62
Cologne, 14, 57, 61
Colouring methods, 38–47, 66–71
Colour-twist, *see* stem technique
Compagnie des Cristalleries de Baccarat, 124
Constantine the Great (Emp.), 14, 61
Core technique, 31
Cork Glass Co., 113
Corning Glass Works, 120
Corning Museum, 96, 102
Coty, Monsieur, 128
Couper, James & Sons, 114
Cristallai, 73
Cristallo, 16, 35, 75
Cristallo-ceramie, 40–1
Crackle glass manufacture, 44
Crizzling, 18, 34
Cros, Henri, 128
Crown glass manufacture, 32

Crutched Friars, 96
Crystallization, 34
Cullet, 24–5
Cutting technique, 49–50, 66
Czechoslovakia, 80, 88, 148

Dagnia family, 93, 97, 104, 111
Dagnia-Williams, 112
Damascus, 12, 14, 16, 45, 65–6, 71
Dammouse, 128
Daum Brothers, 127, 129
Darius I (Emp.), 57
Deckelpokal, 82–3
Decoration methods, 14–16, 39–40, 42–6, 50
Décorchemont, 128
Defects, 18, 34, 36
Denmark, 80, 135; *see also* Scandinavia
Dennis, 115
Devitrification, 34
Diamond stippling process, 50
Dietrata, *see* Cage-cups
Dipstick, 31
Dolny Polubny, 87
Dordrecht, 92
Drams, 109
Dresden, 71, 86
Dublin, 113
Dutch, *see* Holland
Dyottville Glass Works, 117

Ecole de Nancy, 49, 126
Edinburgh, 114
Edkins, Michael, 20, 111, 139
Edwards Belfast (factory), 113
Egermann, Friedrich (Bedrich), 45, 87, 143
Egypt, 12–14, 30, 49, 52, 53–7
Eindhoven, 92
Elgin Vase, 159
Elizabeth I (Eng. queen), 96
Enamel glass, 38
Enamelling process, 35, 45–6; Transparent, 86–7
Enamel-twist, *see* stem technique
England, 14, 22–3, 41–2, 45, 49, 67–9, 80, 83, 93–117, 119, 121, 122, 124, 134, 139, 140, 144, 146, 148, 154; *see also* Britain
Engraving process, 49–50
Ennion, 56, 57
Epinay, 124
Etching process (Acid), 50–1
Europe, 14, 49, 57, 61, 66, 67, 90, 117–19, 131, 138–40, 144, 146–7
Exeter, 68
Exeter flute, 91, 99
Exeter Museum, 99

170

INDEX

Hurdals Verk, 135-6
Hyalith glass, 87-8

Iceglass manufacture, 44
Igel, 78
Industrial Art Museum, Prague, 82
Innsbruck, 80
Intaglio, 50, 55, 83-4
Ireland, 111, 112, 119, 140
Iridescence, 36
Islam, 12, 14, 22, 23, 45, 61-6, 130, 141
Israel, 141
Italy, 12, 13, 55, 56, 58, 66, 69-70, 72, 75, 77, 80, 82, 121, 132, 134, 149
Izmailova, 132

Jachymov, 79
Jackson, Francis, 108
Jacobite symbols, 110-11, 112, 147, 152
Jacobs family, 111
Jacobsz, Adam *and* Willem, 92
James II (Eng. k.), 80
Jamestown, Va., 21, 117
Japan, 127
Jason, 56
Jasper ware, 113
Jenny Lind bottles, 155
Jerusalem, 14
John Akerman & Son, 110
John of Utynam, 42
Justinian (Emp.), 62

Kaltmalerei, 46
Kamenicky Senov, 80, 88
Karl (Landgrave), 84
Kassel, 84
Keith, James, 135
Kensington, Pa., 117
Kerch, 22, 56
Kiev, 64, 132
Killinger, Georg Friedrich, 83
King's College Chapel, Cambridge, 68
King's Lynn, 68, 97, 108
Kitcat glasses, 107
Knop types, 102-3
Kny, Frederick, 115
Koepping, 89
Koet, Elias, 132
Köhler, Heinrich Gottlieb, 135
Kolovrat, Count, 81
König, Joseph Palme, 120
Kosta factory, 136
Kostroma, 132
Kothgasser, Anton, 71, 87, 138
Krasniy Gigant, 133
Krautstrunk, 78

Kreybich, George Francis, 80
Kuantung, 134
Kunckel, G. E., 85
Kunckel, Johann, 20, 38, 85; *Ars vitraria experimentalis*, 47, 86
Kungsholm Glassbruk factory, 134
Kuttrolf (Angster), 58, 79

Lace-glass, 42
Lacy-glass, 118
Ladle, 29
La Ferrière, 121
La Granja de San Ildefonso, 131
Lalique, René, 128-9
Latticinio, 42-3
Lauensteiner Hütte, 84
Laxenburg, 71
Lead glass, 17, 35, 101
Leighton, W., 153
Léveillé-Rousseau, 128
Leyden, 92
Lehman, Caspar, 19, 49-50, 82, 84
Liège, 14, 30, 76, 90, 94-5
Lipper, 29
Lisle, Anthony de, 97
Lithyalin glass, 45
Lloyd, William, 55
Lobmeyr, J., 120
Lobmeyr, Louis, 88, 120
Lomonosov, M. V., 132
London, 68, 80, 83, 97, 104, 110, 138, 156-7
London Glass Sellers' Company, 17-18
London Museum, 99, 151, 157
Longueval, G. F. A., 87-8
Lorraine, 14, 33, 42, 69, 89, 95-6
Lötz Witwe, 89, 120
Louis XIII (Fr. k.), 123
Louis XIV (Fr. k.), 122
Louis XV (Fr. k.), 124
Louis C. Tiffany Co., 119
Low Countries; *see* Netherlands; Belgium; Holland
Lucas, John Robert, 113-14
Lucas, Richard, 122
Luck of Edenhall (beaker), 45, 65
Ludwell, Dr., 35
Ludwig, Philip, Count, 64
Lullo, Bishop, 15
Lycurgus cup, 60
Lynn glass, 108

Maigelein, 79
Mainz, 14
Maltzev, 132-3
Mandarin glass, 134

INDEX

INDEX